The War Diaries of Colin Dunford Wood

Volume 1
Soldier to Airman

The North-West Frontier, India and Iraq
1939-41

Edited by

James Dunford Wood

Published by
Kensington Square

For Colin's grandchildren.

Colin Dunford Wood on the day he passed out from Sandhurst, 1938.

Contents

Introduction

MY FATHER, COLIN DUNFORD WOOD, kept his diary (of which this is the first of three volumes) continuously from early 1939 to the time of the Indian Partition in 1947.

This first volume contains a unique record of two little-known campaigns: the fight against the Fakir of Ipi on the North West Frontier before the war; and a rare first-hand account of the Siege and Battle of Habbaniya, an episode that came very close to driving a wedge through the heart of the British Empire at one of the most perilous junctures of its history.

After graduating from Sandhurst in 1938, he arrived in India to join the Leicestershire Regiment on the North West Frontier in Waziristan, and when war broke out, he was posted to the 13th Frontier Force Rifles in Madras. However, he soon got frustrated. His brother Hugh was flying Blenheim bombers in England, while he was stuck, as he saw it, in an Indian Army backwater. So in mid-1940 he started to take flying lessons, and volunteered to join the RAF.

But there was a problem: his eyesight was less than perfect and he had to fly with specially adapted goggles. However, as he recounts in these pages, he cheated on the eye test and got himself accepted for the 4th Intermediate Flight Training School at RAF Habbaniya, Iraq. As he was later to say - 'from the frying pan into the fire.'

Because although RAF Habbaniya was considered a quiet posting, far from the front line, it very soon became the front line after Rashid Ali's coup in Baghdad in April 1941. Suddenly Britain's oil supply, and its lines of communication, were in jeopardy, and all that stood between the Iraqis and their German reinforcements were 39 trainee pilots and their instructors of the flying school in antiquated biplanes. My father was one of them. The story he tells in these pages is astonishing.

This volume ends with the final victory, though of the three Indian army officers who transferred to the RAF alongside Colin, only one would survive the battle.

Volumes Two and Three cover his no less colourful RAF career in Burma, China, Egypt and Europe, flying Lysanders, Hurricanes and Spitfires. He flew the last Hurricane out of Burma before the advancing Japanese, and flew in support of the Allied armies crossing the Rhine.

These diaries are a vivid portrait of war across several continents and campaigns. Rather than follow the ordered chronology of the tidy historian, who has points to make and theories to prove, the narrative follows the haphazard progress of war on the ground and in the air – encompassing fear, boredom, incompetence, luck, romance, and horror – all interlaced with a self-deprecating humour that kept the man sane.

What's also revealing about them is how his outlook on life changes as he grows up against the background of war. From a naive 20-year-old on the North West Frontier in 1939, raring to go and desperate for action, but still unsure of himself, he rapidly gains confidence in the social whirl of Madras, together with an irreverent attitude to authority that will stand him in good stead in adventures to come. This proved to be one of the happiest periods of the war for him, an endless round of parties and girls and fun, where for the first time he finds himself accepted with open arms. But it's still adventure he craves, and when he finally achieves his mission, somewhat under false pretences, and gets himself transferred to the RAF in Habbaniya - *'how long will this wheeze last?'* - he is quickly pitched into more than he bargained for.

Diaries of this sort are relatively rare, not least because it was forbidden for soldiers and airmen on the front line to record what they saw. They are even rarer in that he also faithfully recorded what he saw with his camera, to accompany the text.

They are full of military expressions, slang and abbreviations, strange place names (occasionally transcribed inaccurately by me and often spelt wrong in the first place by my father), and on occasion snippets of Urdu, Hindi and Pashto. To decipher these, I have added a glossary at the end. Where I have made errors I would be delighted to be corrected, and if anyone knows the meanings or origin of any unfamiliar terms, please feel free to let me know!

James Dunford Wood, London, January 2023.

Part 1

1st Battalion
Leicestershire Regiment

The North-West Frontier

January 2nd 1939

Razani

WE MARCH DOWN TO RAZANI TODAY, TWELVE MILES. We head the column, which includes some other units including the 2/4 Gurkha Rifles We have two picquets to put out, below the Nazri on the left. A snowstorm comes on, and chaps put on their jerkins, but I have not brought mine. I am wearing full pack and haversack, and it strains the shoulders.

At Greenwood's Corner, the Battalion takes a shortcut down the Kud, which is tricky going for the mules. At the bottom of the road there's an icy surface, and one mule is down and unable to get up, the others queuing up behind. We pass on and eventually reach Razani. There's a full stand-to until the C.O. comes round and everything is settled.

Razani is a Battalion camp with a stone perimeter, with six numbered picquets on the surrounding hills, and one up near Melozai. Wana huts are the quarters, and most are dug down, some especially for officers, to head level. This is for protection against snipers.

The 3/14 Punjabis have very kindly moved out into the Brigade camp, ordinarily holes and mule lines, which is now full up, including the 2/4 Gurkha Rifles. The 3/14 and 2/4 are going on to Dandil on the 3rd to take part in a Khaisora column. We have to put up another tent as an anteroom - there's not enough room in the mess for fifteen officers, as well as feed.

Gunga Din[1] unpacks. I have a camp bed, a lilo, and four blankets. I forgot a pillow, so use a pair of greyers. The bed is near the door, and I freeze all night.

---

[1] Colin's nickname for his bearer. 'Gunga Din' is one of Rudyard Kipling's best-known poems. It features two characters, the speaker who is a British soldier fighting in India, and Gunga Din, an Indian water carrier.

Razani camp

January 3rd 1939

RAZANI

RECCE PATROL DOWN TO KHAISORA CROSSING, to let the Brigade through to Dandil. I am wearing chaplis[1] for a first tryout. My platoon picquets Lower Tambre Obo, an old built-up camp picquet, with the remains of a perimeter camp below it, overlooking the head of the Khaisora. A pretty dangerous-looking place, surrounded by nullahs (dry riverbed, ravine) whose beds are out of sight. In front is another platoon on Upper Tambre Obo, overlooking the village. The Green Howards had seven casualties on the Maidan on our left, whilst going up to Mamha Roga. Captain Ainsley was killed up there too. Clarke arrives up, as officer commanding D company, with a bottle of beer. I have just got it open when I get caught with returning fire. However, the platoon scrambles down, under cover of the VB[2] which I sent down to the old campsite, across the Khaisora and up a precipitous bank on the other side.

3

I reckon chaplis beat boots any day, except perhaps in snow. Recce patrol in future is done by gashts *(Urdu: promenade/ inspection patrol or survey on foot - see the Glossary at the end of the book)*. Patrols of three or four platoons go out and leapfrog from hill to hill, parallel to the road, hoping to catch a Dushman (local word for an enemy). There's Khasadar picquet, Morton's Bump (after a lad in 3/14), 72, 71, and Knife Edge. Up the other way, it's more dangerous, with two villages, Razani and Zargaran.

We did a wonderful gasht up there to reconnoitre Zorgat Algad and it looks pretty grim, with a ruined village. I was holding a shale crest and took a section down the side of Zargaran to hold a position looking up towards Zorgat Algad, to cover a platoon. I needed a bodyguard with fixed bayonets as protection from fierce dogs, but the threat of a stone seemed quite sufficient.

Life in Razani when there's no patrolling is pretty dull, but we have a seven-a-side football league in which I play. The Gunners win that. Officers vs Sergeants on a Sunday morning and beer afterwards. Most enjoyable. Dick Forsythe is one of the gunners, Captain Guy Lambert is the other officer. Dick arrived in India last Easter, went to Hyderabad and Sind, and has been here eight weeks. Brigade HQ is at Nowshara, and has a section at Dandil. He goes off to Mir Ali after a bit, with all the rest of the gunners, and I take over Sally, a labrador belonging to the Adjutant of 3/14. I have her for about two weeks and am charged R7/12, for 1lb meat per diem @ 4 annas. I wrote to Captain Harvey about it.

I took up a squad and built a cookhouse up at No 4 picquet and did general repairs. Then the main well fell in on the cookhouse and the cook claims he was there, which I don't believe. In excavations, we find two unbroken eggs. Eventually Clarke has to revet with 16ft angle irons and corrugated iron, or the whole post would collapse.

I am pretty ill for three days, following a cold, with a chill on the liver and violent indigestion. Eventually I go up in a staff car on 29th January and roll down to the hospital to find I have catarrhal jaundice. I go back to my quarters and arrange a change of bearers.

Gunga Din gets my goat, always looking as though he had just had his pants kicked. Major Brain 6/13 got me the brother of his, one Attam Khan, a Pathan from near Peshawar. He arrives down at Razani with blankets around him like a tribesman, and I stammer Urdu at him and send him back up, as I am going to Razmak the next day. The handover is completed, and I move into the hospital.

February 10th 1939

RAZMAK

I AM PRONOUNCED BILE FREE AND ADVISED TO GET UP, as I'll soon be discharged. This is the thirteenth day in hospital and I'm about fed up. It was a nice rest at first, between sheets after four weeks in Razani, but a fat-free diet is very monotonous - soup and jelly predominant. The only thing I got my teeth into was toast and jam. Later comes promotion to boiled chicken and mutton and fruit salad. Breakfast is grape nuts, Force and two boiled eggs.

There's a very pleasant Assistant Surgeon here, Irving, and a Major looking just like something off the stage. I move in with Field for a bit who has been evacuated with some sort of flu. He goes out pretty soon. Captain Fowler, who succeeded Murray as the Doctor at Razani, looks in and says that a gang of Badmashes with a gun were reported between Khaisora and Razani.

Much shooting in Razani the other day, but only two villagers chasing a duck. Whilst I was there we had no shooting, the last being about Christmas, but they usually snipe when the Brigade is in camp there.

The picquets got windy one night and blew off all sorts of coloured Very lights at about 7.30 pm in the rain. Someone heard a noise in Nullah picquet, which guards a well. Nullah 685 all let off.

And our No 3 post too, thinking they saw someone just outside the wall. But only an Indian at the latrines.

They sacked 100 Khasadars up at Razmak Narai. The orderlies are pretty idle here, being the King's, up from Peshawar to relieve ours, as we are short of men. We have been up here three months without a shot fired at us; save two or three which landed on my platoon's sangars (sangar: an observation post) on patrol. Of course, I was in Nowshara, dammit.

A column went out Makin way just before Christmas, I had a platoon up Gibraltar to cover them. A colossal battle they have at Tandi China corner. I hear guns, VBs and MGs. They come home with about twenty casualties. Two men are shot dead in Shora picquet, by the red fort. Whilst we are down in Razani, they shoot up some recce troops in Razmak.

There is the famous occasion in early December when the lad near Bakkoke picquet lets off thirty or forty shots at gunners mules returning from patrol. They lose two mules, and lots of artillery open on him. No good. Later that evening he moves around and puts a few into the camp - 6/13 lines and 2/7 Rajputs. One of the perimeter posts has V.B. trained on where he is believed to have been. They didn't open up as they were not risking punishment. Bloody fools.

Maybe it's the old custom of watching a new unit, watching it first keen, then going slack (familiarity breeds contempt) and eventually someone buys it. I hope it won't be me.

The 2nd Brigade including the Royal Ulster Rifles has moved up to Bannu, but it may only be normal relief of 1st Brigade. Rumour has it that they go to the lower end of Khaisora, and the 1st Brigade, who are now back in Dandil, take the upper end. It's also rumoured the Leicesters remain in Razani until 2/12 come as relief of 3/14 on March 15th. The 6/13 hung their shield last night and the first casualty comes down this morning - a Major Allan RIASC, who got hit by a bottle or some'at and broke his "eye film".

I have trouble getting books from the Club babu. I sent for his catalogue, and he swore he hadn't one, eventually relenting and letting me have it two days later, when I'd asked Fowler to call in and order it. I chose some books, got 'em, but next time he claimed they were all out. I'll sort him when I get up there.

Intelligence reports that Ipi is trying for a Holy War, when his pals have returned from the Plains. Also rumours of declaring operations, and Brain says they are giving a medal for 1938 and that we shall be eligible. Had a letter from Biddy Benbow, wanting a photo of me, and one from Bill[1] having taken six days only. I thought it took that to Karachi alone. He has no opinion of Arabs, "Oozlebats" or Jews, but hasn't had a battle yet. Nor have I for that matter. The troops reckon the Green Howards were pulling their legs. They got pitched straight into war when they arrived, whilst we have had three months calm, for training. I heard that the bushman who shot up the gate so long ago was ambushed by two Gurkhas and they chopped his hands off. Maybe. I also hear they got the chap who sniped Razmak, whilst we have been away, over by HMS Nelson, a factory chimney and incinerator. His fate I suppose will be six months jug, and when he's let out I believe they give him 50 chips to start life anew. It's so damn silly, he should be charged with attempted murder, or treason, as I believe he was a Khasadar *(local militia)*.

[1] *Colin's best friend Bill Robinson, based in Palestine.*

February 11th 1939

RAZMAK

I AM UP AND WALKING ABOUT FOR TWO DAYS NOW. Captain Fowler comes up and says he is treating a Khasadar who got shot in the Razani shooting the other day. On the second attempt, he got a bullet out of the Khasadar's foot, also some gravel and small stones, so reckons it must have been a ricochet. Pallot, who is acting adjutant up here, tells me there passed through his hands a request from 1/12 for a report on me. Lt Col Lockhart actually. I had thought that was a dead letter now. However, Quien Sabe? Major Allan got hit by a jerry whilst playing rugger in the club, and I believe there were one or two other casualties too.

First day on a normal diet of fats. Saw Tundan[1] in the bazaar. He was seen in Razani with an armband with BF on it; when questioned, so the story goes, he said "Brigade Photographer". He says he can't publish photos in the press, without getting Brigade's sanction which, he says, takes a month, by which time the photos no longer have any news value. Small hopes for me; there might be court-martials and all. I reckon I'm not yet bile-free, as there are deposits about midday. There is much rain lately, especially at night, so perhaps the snow is over, although Irving says it isn't warm here until April. District HQ moves up here, because in D.I.Khan it goes up to 120 degrees. The wind here is known colloquially as the "Sting of Death" and it certainly lives up to its reputation.

I'm sick of the picture, framed, squatting on the mantelpiece - "The man who missed on the first tee at St Andrews".

[1] A local photographer. (B.R. Tundan was a civilian photographer on the North West frontier, whose images were widely printed for use by British troops).

February 13th 1939

Razmak

A STRANGE INCIDENT LAST NIGHT. At about 11.45 pm there is a noise of someone letting off his rifle continuously, pretty close, and gradually getting further away, as though he were running off down the road. At first I thought it was in the compound, and eventually I dismissed it as some lad letting off fireworks to celebrate. But no, Irving swears it was shooting and that some of the shots hit the MO's mess and officer's quarters. It beats me.

THE MAN WHO MISSED THE BALL ON THE FIRST TEE AT ST. ANDREWS

Today I visit the dentist for a stopping. I see in the Statesman that on the night of February 5th/6th a Madda Khel lashkar[1] let off fifteen shots from 800 feet with a gun at Datta Khel fort. Two penetrated the walls, and eventually an aeroplane from Miramshah dispersed the gang at 2.45 am by moonlight.

One Assistant Surgeon here, an Anglo-Indian, had his own private practice at Razani, amongst the tribesmen, whom he treated in return for chicken and eggs. That's a regular occurrence, apparently, except with a British MO.

[1] Lashkars were rebel tribesmen, this one of the Madda Khel tribe.

February 15th 1939

Razmak

THIS MORNING DAWNS WITH SIX INCHES OF SNOW, and it is continually a steady downpour. I have had two teeth stopped and go today for a final polish. I hear the 1st Brigade went out yesterday, down the Khaisora. To join the 2nd Brigade I suppose.

The Faqir of Ipi

Ghazi Mirzali Khan Wazir, commonly known as the Faqir of Ipi, was a Pashtun tribal leader and holy man from Waziristan, an area bordering the North West Frontier province of British India and the non-administered tribal territory straddling the border with Afghanistan. This was, and remains, one of the most remote and anarchic places on earth, whose inhabitants have long cherished a fierce independence from any form of 'civilised' government. Ipi, a 1930's Osama Bin Laden, waged guerrilla warfare against the British Empire from 1936 until the British left in 1947, and, unlike Bin Laden, remained undefeated. Initially based in the village of Ipi, he subsequently relocated to caves near Gurwek, a remote village in North Waziristan on the border with Afghanistan. It was here that he declared an independent state - Pashtunistan - in 1937.

The initial cause of his rebellion was the interference of a British Indian court in the forced marriage and conversion to Islam of a Hindu girl in Bannu. The verdict in her favour enraged the Pashtuns, and Ipi succeeded in uniting the local Wazir tribes and raise a rebellion of 10,000 in the Khaisora Valley. The Pashtun rebels, including women as well as men, blocked roads, overran outposts, attacked picquets and ambushed convoys. In November 1936, the British sent two columns to the Khaisora valley to crush the rebellion, but suffered heavy casualties. Following this, they brought up two squadrons of aircraft, and pursued a campaign of scorched earth from the air, burning villages with petrol bombs and killing cattle with strafing attacks. On New Year's Eve 1936, the RAF bombed one of his remote hideaways in Arsal Kot while an infantry brigade, about 3,000 strong with light tanks, pushed up the virtually impassable valleys under constant sniper fire.

But after storming the lair they found eight caves, grouped on either side of a deep gorge, untouched from the fighting - and empty. It was said that Ipi slipped through a cordon of Frontier Scouts with his head wrapped in a sheet.

Unsurprisingly, the Fakir of Ipi quickly gained a mystical reputation in India - it was said his religious powers would protect his followers from bombs and bullets. The British estimated he could call on over 100,000 fighting men, and that his effective fighting force never dipped below 10,000 lashkars, with access to over 20,000 modern rifles, many manufactured by small gun factories set up in the villages of the tribal lands. Indeed, he was feted by the British themselves, who nicknamed him the 'Scarlet Pimpernel of Waziristan' - "They sought him here, they sought him there, those columns sought him everywhere."

The Waziristan insurgency was the only place throughout the Empire in the late 1930s where British officers could gain combat experience, and it got a reputation as a place of high adventure, much prized as a first posting by officers, such as Colin, graduating from Sandhurst.

Having failed to capture Ipi or bomb him into submission with their expeditionary forces and air campaigns, the British decided in 1937 to permanently garrison the area, in a new 'Forward Frontier' policy. 40,000 British-Indian troops, mostly Sikhs from the Punjab led by British officers, were based in Razmak, Bannu and Wanu. In response to an ambush by Waziristani tribesmen in which they killed over fifty British soldiers (including fifteen officers) - the Shahur Tangi ambush (see p. 29 for a description) - the British attempted to subdue the area through columns launched from their cantonments and picqueting on the hills, but they failed to quell the uprising and, with a constant stream of casualties, they eventually retreated to camp, concentrating instead on imposing fines and destroying the houses of the rebel leaders. This retreat was seized upon by the rebels as a great victory for Ipi, whose reputation soared, and he was soon being courted by the Italian and German legations in Kabul, who saw a way to destabilise the British. They offered him money and guns, some of which got through, but fortunately for the British, Ipi was disinclined to make an alliance with any foreign power, and he continued on his singular but highly effective guerilla campaign, at his own pace.

11

Finallly, tired of their inability to capture him, the British offered him a pardon and ceasefire in 1938, but he rejected it. He continued harassing the British, tying up valuable Indian divisions, throughout the war, and once the British left in 1947, he continued his struggle for independence against the newly created state of Pakistan.

He died peacefully in his bed in 1960, and his obituary in the Times described him as a "doughty and honourable opponent, a man of principle and saintliness, a redoubtable organiser of tribal warfare."

The Brigadier came in yesterday, after presenting Irving with his L.S. and G.C. medal. Andrews's "Challenge of the North West Frontier" puts forward some interesting opinions. Russia is no longer a menace, being occupied with her own undeveloped Asiatic territory, and faced with a German-Japan axis. India pays for the British troops out here, has no say in their employment, takes orders from Britain in the League of Nations, so we obtain two votes and seats there. He reckons there's no justification for keeping such a large army on the frontier. It's an Imperial reserve, no doubt, paid for by India, but our Waziristan policy seems a failure, and so many troops only irritate the tribesmen. He advocates a withdrawal, and the establishment of medical centres, as a beginning of peaceful administration. Air bombing, even with warning, seems to be just as barbarous in the actual results obtained, driving the homeless tribesmen to the rifle as a means of subsistence.

But they are responsible for raids on the plains or into Afghanistan - surely adequate border patrols and posts would keep the Plains safe? Maybe the Chatfield commission will have far-reaching developments and suggestions to put forward in their report. But Peter Fleming's account of Russian activities in Sinkiang seems to bear out the old bogey.[1]

[1] *News From Tartary, published 1936.*

February 16th 1939

Razmak

ABOUT FOURTEEN INCHES OF SNOW. They say that that gun was tried out on Datta Khel again, a few days ago, and blew up, taking three dushmen with it.

Had a talk with Major Allan. Razcol last year had 32 killed and 97 wounded, on what were 'Peace' columns. The Green Howards were asked why they used field dressings on peace columns. They replied that they had some casualties and were then, so he says, asked to state their authority for having casualties on peace columns!

The new well behind Somme lines was found by an RIASC officer, a water diviner. He used a twig, or a piece of wire. Major Allan was shown how to use it, and got a distinct tremor over a small burn. He came up with the original occupation troops in 1923, and was horrified at my description of the troops getting browned off, saying it was the old, old story, and we should buy it sooner or later.

Lord Chatfield was shown some mountain howitzers at Dandil, and asked how they were transported. When told on a mule, he exclaimed "But you can't get that on a mule!" He never realised that they were taken to pieces! After all his service, even though a naval officer. I am due for discharge tomorrow, being the 20th day of incarceration.

February 19th 1939

Razmak

I SEE THE BACK INTELLIGENCE REPORTS TODAY. Datta Khel seems to have been besieged for about a week. The gun that blew up was a 2.75" of local make, firing explosive shells. Mirali also seems to have been sniped pretty frequently, and all that upper Tochi area seems to be in a turmoil. Ipi is trying to get help from both sides of the border, and is receiving cash from the sale of animal skins, slaughtered for Id. All the recent sniping of Razmak and patrols is put down to the dismissed Tori Khel Khasadars. I think they were dismissed because their section of the Tori Khel failed to turn in the local outlaws who they were harbouring.

I play squash with Major James, then we go down to say goodbye to the 6/13. Brain is there and a lot of the 5/11. The proofs of my photographs are not very good, so I will go down tomorrow and get them done again.

Officer's lines at Razmak camp in winter.

February 20th 1939

RAZMAK

THERE HAS BEEN NO MAIL FOR TWO DAYS, but it has stopped snowing today, and they are snow clearing, so it ought to get up today. My sea boots are a godsend. There's absolutely nothing to do up here. Saw Wallace Beery in "The Bad Man of Brimstone" the other night, which I missed seeing at home. It was on in Chester, when I changed there on my way to stay with Jonah.

Attam Khan (Colin's bearer) is doing pretty well, and my room looks as though it has been done up when I return from hospital. Feeding in the Club is very good and all for Rs 3/- a day. There are a few RIASC majors who mess there, and the Padre, two RCs, a Veterinary officer and an engineer too. Azarrepo has just come back from down the Jandola road. There is a scout post of 300 at Sarroga, and they apparently have fifteen "hostages" there. These are near relations of local badmashes, and they are in a sort of concentration camp receiving eight annas a day. If the badmashes

Khasadars, Lashkars and Khels

Before the British arrived, the hill-based frontier tribes survived by raiding the fertile valleys in summer. Their own stony hillsides were barren, and apart from some sheep, did not yield much of a living. So in order to keep them quiet, and to persuade them to cease raiding across the border into the administered areas, the British paid the tribal chiefs a stipend to keep the peace and 'render services' such as guard roads and camps. This cash grant amounted to one million rupees in 1939. In return, the tribal chiefs supplied manpower to undertake these tasks, called khasadars. (See opposite - the photograph was taken either by Colin or Arora, the local Army photographer, and a print bought by Colin.).

Cleverly, though, the chieftains tended to supply young boys and elderly men, all pre- or post fighting age, which meant that they retained a fighting force of fit young men should the need arise. These khasadars were often fairly useless. Whenever the Faqir of Ipi launched a raid, or when they were launched by the tribes (contrary to the agreement), these khasadars tended to melt away.

A lashkar refers to a rebel tribesman or a group of them - the young men of fighting age who remained to carry on what they had always done: fighting and scrapping with their neighbours, and with any outside power that attempted to subdue them. The tribal clans and villages they belonged to were called Khels.

misbehave, the "hostages" are put in the jug, receiving only three annas. All this seems damn silly, but I can't fathom the policy of the political administrator here. The hostages smuggled in with them two small boys to provide light entertainment.

That gun that blew up at Datta Khel was found by a scouting patrol. At least, they found the barrel and breech block, a large pool of blood and a man's ear. The site was also well marked by MG fire from the post, so they weren't far out. Letters from Uncle George and Mrs Robinson.

February 26th 1939
RAZMAK

CONTINUOUS SNOW ON AND OFF, for the whole week practically now. The mountain tops look rather grim when you see them outlined in a gap in the smokey grey mist which swirls about their base. They seem to sort of loom out of the mist, especially with the sun behind them. I met a Sikh, clad in a pair of pants, outside his barrack room, giving himself a bath with the aid of soap and cold water in an oil tin, the whole thing swept by an icy snow-laden wind.

The political administrator said the sniper was caught at HMS Nelson, was a small boy, with a rifle about the length of your arm, who said he was potting pigeons. The Masudha brought him in, and he is to be tried by a Jirga. *(An assembly of elders.)*

February 27th 1939
RAZMAK

I GOT ORDERS TO REJOIN RAZANI YESTERDAY. That's a bit of a blow, as I had intended visiting the 5/13 on March 3rd. However, it snowed a foot or so in the night so I am snowbound up here today.

Waziris at a tribal jirga, image by Arora.

February 28th 1939

RAZMAK

STILL SNOWING. RAZANI POSTPONED until Friday for some reason. I pay Attam Khan today, and when it is all settled he takes a look at it and asks what he is going to get next month. I tell him the same, and then he breaks out about the Major sahib giving him 35/- and 10/- for the contract. I say all very well but I'm not a Major sahib yet, nor drawing a Major sahib's pay, but when I transfer to the Indian army I will give him a rise. He has to be content with that.

I took a walk around the wall yesterday, at least I waded round and at the 2/1 G. lines I came upon a snow fight. I potted Seaward, was ambushed, and then joined in. The enemy were Sikh gunners living opposite. I broke one window and tried to hit some spectators at open windows but no good. I received one right down the throat, almost choking over it.

It's a queer site to look along one of the roads with an exit gate at its end, especially if slightly uphill. The white nothingness at the end gives the impression of it being a sort of pier head. Reminiscent

SKETCH MAP OF ROAD R2K. - RKN.
SHOWING PICQUET POSITIONS.
SCALE: 1" = 1 mile approx.

66

RKN

X DAS

67

X TOC

DUN
X

X NULLAH
68

X TOADY

X PINK HILLS

X CROCOS

69

X 7101

X 7022

70

X NULLAH

X TOWER

X HORSESHOE.

CAJ
X

.6994
(OAK).

71

X HOLLY

X GOAT.

P.E. Wing
1/LE109
14/9/

of Tiree. I see in the intelligence of India that all Pathan militiamen in the 4/2 have been discharged, as their services could no longer be relied upon. The Pathan quarter guard did nothing about the incident, and it was a Pathan who shot up the British officers. One Royal Ulster Regiment lad wounded the other day in Khaisora.

March 2nd 1939
Razmak

I GO OUT DOG SHOOTING with the Provost Sergeant, and Carey as well, and we shoot four pie dogs. Three in the 5/11 Officers lines, which won't go down too well, as we left the bodies lying there by the side of the path. Whilst out on the Jandola road, outside No 2. gate, I slip in my sea boots on the icy surface and break the stock of my gun and also the spectacle lens in my hip pocket. A damn silly thing to do. The Provost Sergeant said that about three weeks ago two 6/11 Jawas, carting out refuse just beyond HMS Razmak, were caught and stripped of everything, being sent back starko with their mules.

He also said some Chinamen operated a gambling den in the skating rink and several chaps lost up to Rs 200/-. One sportsman decided to take his revenge, as when he had returned to ask for Rs 10/- or so back for fags, he was thrown out. One night, whilst going to shut the bazaar, the Provost Sergeant saw a match striking close to the ground by the skating rink walls. He leapt over the wire, and the fellow got away but he found the walls petrol-soaked, breast-high.

March 5th 1939
Razani

HAD A LAST EVENING'S DOG SHOOT before coming down here on the 3rd. Badly hit one pie behind the abattoir, and I blew up another one in Borretts Park, but not much game out. James drove us down and we had a look at his well in the nullah.

Yesterday I went on a gasht and it rained with occasional snow, but I had a ground sheet which kept most of it off. The route was 72, 72 forward, Peacock Tree, and then Miller and I were ordered up to Zawata Manza ridge. This is "ungashted" country, and a bloody place to get up. About four or five nullahs seem to converge at the foot of a knife edge, and we could have been enfiladed out of sight of the MG covering fire. A Tochi scout picquet was at the top - keen-looking fellows squatting motionless with their rifles behind rocks. How different from the British soldier! They never moved, and hardly spoke.

One of the machine gunners on guard last night shot himself in the thigh with his revolver. He saw a bit of rust on the hammer and cocked it to clean it off. It went off and then exploded. It also must have been a dud charge, as the bullet broke the bone and is lodged in the leg. No marks of burning either. He was a Grimsby man, and claims he was so excited about Grimsby Town winning their cup match, that the accident happened.[1]

[1] *They beat Chelsea 1-0 in the 6th round of the FA Cup on March 4th, then went on to lose the FA Cup semi-finals to Wolves on March 25th.*

March 7th 1939

RAZANI

YESTERDAY I'M CAUGHT WITH THE "GENERAL ALARM" at 1 am, and get as far as the M.I. room on my way to the lines, in rubber boots and overcoat, before I realise what a bloody fool I am.

On a gasht yesterday. No. 7 picquet, along 70 ridge, Gardai camp, No. 72 and home. It is very pleasant down by Gardai camp, having crossed the nullah. A sound of a small burn in the nullah bed, an up convoy crossing the Khaisora, sounding like the roar of the sea.

I fancy I hear a sheep bleat, and I am back in Tiree. All very pleasant. Several loose camels can be seen grazing behind a flock of goats.

March 8th 1939

RAZANI

GOOD GASHT TODAY – No. 7, No. 74, Gardai, and then searched the ground overlooking Shini Alghad, where it joins the Khairsora. There was a Khasadar on No. 72 with a naik's stripes (Indian army corporal), who said he could arrange shooting up and down for Chakor (a bird) and Khargosh (rabbit), which latter were "so high", he said, putting his hand to the ground and sticking his fingers out from his ears like an elf. This is a rare opportunity, though I can't say I have ever seen one there. There is much aerial bombing, on and off for a week or so, and loud sounds from Mami Rohga way.

March 10th 1939

BANNU

AN RIASC CAPTAIN IS DETAINED at Razani with his convoy. He gives me a lift to Bannu on a lorry, the remainder knocking off at Mir Ali. It was an open sort of lorry, no windscreen, only a bit of tarpaulin to cover your knees. The rain came in, hit the back of the cab, and formed a large puddle which soaked my arse to the skin. I had understood it was essential to leave Bannu by 12.15, so I curse the driver to get me there in time and to go faster - but to no avail.

There is water in the nullah, and green stuff springing up in fields on the banks, a welcome sight. We reach Bagai Bannu depot at about 12.25 but they don't mind, and say the road is open until 4 pm. I seem to remember threatening a tonga wallah with my revolver, to make him get off the road quicker, as I was in such a bloody hurry. Bagai had a beautiful Oldsmobile ready, and off we go to Kohat. That stretch – Bannu-Kohat – is pretty desolate, a salt range looking like sandstone. No vegetation, all this bare red earth. We pass a few police posts, but no sign of R.P. troops or sangars or picquets.

There is a fellow here, Heard of 3/12. He was in Wanu during the Shahur Tangi show[1], and lost one subaltern of about six months service. About six British Officers were killed and nine wounded. A convoy with Wanu pay, and scouts, had passed through the gorge the day before, and they saw all these birds, like vultures, lining the Tangi. They said they were just sitting there watching, beady-eyed. In the Club, some wit said they were bagging who would get who, for future reference. Quite true.

Next day the convoy was told by Khasadars at Manzani that it would be suicide to go on. In the official report, the blame was put on the political agent - "Consequent on the political strategy..." – so off the convoy went and the Tangi wasn't picketed. They were well and truly ambushed. Fire poured in all along the line. A company of Punjabis, as local protection, took to the hills overlooking the Tangi, and did their best. The armoured cars did theirs. After they had finished the slaughter, the tribesmen raided the lorries, took what they wanted (about the only arms were British Officers' revolvers), and left the next morning.

Scouts had arrived the evening before, but could only close picquet the column, so that anyone coming near them went to hell, but could loot the convoy at his leisure. The convoy eventually reached Wana, with whole lorries full of dead, shot in the first volley. The bloody shame was that everyone knew it would happen, yet the convoy was allowed through.

Heard had also seen cheetah hunting – a disgraceful sport. The cheetah is sent after a herd of buck in the manner of a falcon. If well-trained, it tracks down a good stag and holds it down, without breaking its skin. Then the tribesmen slit its belly, having first castrated it, whilst it is still alive, and give the cheetah some blood

'Through the gate: returning to camp'.

from the bowels, apparently the only way to make the cheetah let go.

Went drinking to the Ekins with Hearn. Colonel Ekin seems to think the Bagai and the Mashud contractors pay out half their earnings to the Badmashes to keep the pot boiling. He reckons Razmak, being made up of regular troops instead of scouts, is the wrong principle for Waziristan, and the worst blunder we ever made. He recommends withdrawing to the administrative border, and building a sort of "Taggarts Wall"[2], with troops behind it, and possibly scouts inside the area.

Kohat is rather like Bannu, only smaller, and with magnificent flowers just now. A rather nice bazaar too, natural, and not like Razmak's pseudo-Bond Street.

[1] *An infamous ambush of the Royal Corps of Signals in the Shahur Tangi gorge in 1937.*
[2] *A barbed wire fence erected by the British in Palestine in 1938, to keep militants from infiltrating from Syria to the North. Charles Tegart was an advisor on the suppression of terrorism.*

25

Indian Army Infantry Regiments, 1938

Throughout the diaries there are references to units such as 6/13, 2/12, 3/14 etc. The first number denotes the Battalion (regiments typically had 3-5 Battalions), while the second corresponds to the regiment denominator as below. G.R. is normally added where the text refers to a Gurkha regiment.

1st Punjab Regiment
2nd Punjab Regiment
3rd Madras Regiment
4th Bombay Grenadiers
5th Mahratta Light Infantry
6th Rajputana Rifles
7th Rajput Regiment
8th Punjab Regiment
9th Jat Regiment
10th Baluch Regiment
11th Sikh Regiment
12th Frontier Force Regiment
13th Frontier Force Rifles
14th Punjab Regiment
15th Punjab Regiment
16th Punjab Regiment
17th Dogra Regiment
18th Royal Garhwal Rifles
19th Hyderabad Regiment
20th Burma Rifles
1st King George V's Gurkha Rifles
2nd King Edward's Gurkha Rifles
3rd Queen Alexandra's Gurkha Rifles
4th Prince of Wales's Gurkha Rifles
5th Royal Gurkha Rifles
6th Gurkha Rifles
7th Gurkha Rifles
8th Gurkha Rifles
9th Gurkha Rifles
10th Gurkha Rifles

Regiments and detachments based in Waziristan

Waziristan District: HQ Dera Ismail Khan
Detachment, 2/11th Sikh Regiment
Razmak Brigade: HQ Razmak
11th Light Tank Company, RTR
B Squadron, The Scinde Horse
1st Leicestershire Regiment
2/7th Rajput Regiment
3/10th Baluch Regiment
5/11th Sikh Regiment
2/1st Gurkha Rifles
1/8th Gurkha Rifles
25th Mountain Regiment
Bannu Brigade: HQ Bannu
Skinner's Horse
1 Troop, A Squadron, The Scinde Horse
C Squadron, The Scinde Horse
5/1st Punjab Regiment
1/12th Frontier Force Regiment
1/14th Punjab Regiment
The Tochi Scouts (at Miranshah)
2/12th Frontier Force Regiment (at Mir Ali)
1/4th Gurkha Rifles (at Dandil)
Wana Brigade: HQ Wana
A Squadron, The Scinde Horse (at Manzai)
1 Troop, A Squadron, The Scinde Horse (at Wana)
2/2nd Punjab Regiment (at Manzai)
3/8th Punjab Regiment
1/18th Royal Garhwal Rifles
2/3rd Gurkha Rifles
2/8th Gurkha Rifles
The South Waziristan Scouts (at Jandola)

March 13th 1939

I RETURN TO RAZANI TODAY. Hired a car from Modern Motor Works for 45/-. There is a fellow wanting to go Bannu way, so he buys the contract for RS 5/- so that I might have hired him straight for 40/-. He is a Pathan and a wag. He offers me hard-boiled eggs, purchased on the roadside. I try to get the Khasadar to sit on the luggage grid, there being insufficient room in the back seat, and this causes much 'bat' and merriment. It is then explained to me that he may fall off, and anyhow the dushmen will not see him in the car, and may open fire. I think he is a bit windy of being exposed to a chance bullet.

March 17th 1939

Razani

WENT ON A GASHT YESTERDAY. Sugarloaf, Greenwood's Corner, Camel Hump, No. 78, Shoulder and home. There's quite a lot of snow still up there, which soaked my feet in my chapplies (Indian army sandals). Rumour seems to have it that we shall return to Razmak about the 26th, and go out on a column shortly afterwards. The home trooping draft has been postponed again until May. A deck tennis court has been rigged up here, and my "City of Venice" "all in" games stand me in good stead here.

We have a concert the other night. The troops spend most of the evenings singing, and you hear a surprising number of hymns. This country must surely be as far from the imagined India as possible. The hills are all covered in short bushy scrub, and at present, there is not a blade of grass anywhere. It is pleasant to sit up a hill on a warm day and watch the lower heights and nullahs. Traffic on the road, or another picquet going up below you, are like so many ants, although their movements are easily distinguishable.

'Convoy halt at Dandil'. Image by the photographer Tundan, Colin in shorts.

One can easily imagine a dushman lying behind a rock and taking careful aim at one.

I have my confidential report sent down from Razmak. I am 'tactful with Indians, strictly temperate, and rather abrupt.'

March 19th 1939

RAZANI

INTELLIGENCE REPORTS THAT DURING AN ACTION on the 16th in Khaisora, when the 1st Brigade was trying to evict some enemy from caves where they were lurking, (a very difficult and dangerous job by all accounts, as they have no mortars up there), Lt Beale from 3/17 was killed with ten Indian other ranks, along with two British officers wounded, one Indian officer and ten Indian other ranks. The enemy was reported to have 15 dead, 7 expected dead, and 20 were estimated as being wounded.

There are some gunners here, on their way down from Razmak. Apparently the R.U.R. (Royal Ulster Rifles) are a bloodthirsty lot, baying for dead tribesmen. A section was out doing something or other when they observed 15 armed men or so. After some loud discussion, they decided they were "blankety scouts". Just then three shots rang out, the section commander (Cooley, MM) fell with a bullet through the neck, and two others received holes in their Topees. Then they lay down and opened fire, killing six dushmen, the rest presumably fleeing. Not a bad effort.

There is much talk of us returning to Razmak in a few days, and more talk of the concentration of Razcol, so as to go out in April sometime. I only hope to God they do.

March 22nd 1939

Razani

THE 3/17 C.O. WAS STABBED IN THE ARM, and Simon was wounded by a bullet. Those were the two British officers wounded when Lt Beale was killed.

Gasht to Upper Tambre Obo yesterday, by lorry there and back. Had a long talk with my Khasadar, one Halim Khan. He says there will be a war round here in the warm weather, and mentioned a Holy War led by the Tori Khel. He has met Ipi, and says he is a young man with not much beard, who sits in one place all the time and dictates orders to others to do the work. His rifle cost him Rs 100/-, and he showed me a bullet wound between his toes which he got whilst defending a lorry attacked by dushmen in the nullah here. He was a sentry there and claims to have hit two dushmen. They gave us tea on No. 72 and I fox a few Khasadars with the three-card trick.

Talking of cards, one night in Razmak the C.O. was playing bridge and called "Two spades". The bearer who had brought in the drinks said "bahnt achcha" and left, to return with a toothpick. Now every bearer gets a toothpick on the command "Two spades".

March 27th 1939

DID A GASHT DOWN TO LOWER TAMBRE OBO in lorries. Nothing of note, though I fell down a steep slope and skinned my arm. Next day a long gasht up to No. 78 and No. 80. There I met the major (Moriarty) in command of the company of Baluchis in Alexandra picquet. He had not seen anybody for a week, and invited me up for a beer, but there wasn't time.

Some gunners and RIASC came up with several hundred mules, spending the night here on the way. They are with 2 Brigade in the Shaktu. Dushmen in caves were apparently dug in under an overhang, and so could not be got at. Beale, the 3/17 adjutant, crawled along the overhang and peered over, hoping to shoot someone with his revolver. But there were a few more enemy up the nullah, a little further on, and they shot him in the head. The P.A. eventually induced the 12 or so remaining to come out of their cave, saying their lives would be spared. They did, but suddenly one of them stabbed the C.O. in the arm. The Dogras then went in with the bayonet, and massacred the lot.

The Royal Ulsters take over from us on the 30th, when we march back to Razmak. They and 2/1 G.R. have to sit in the old camp for the night, which will be bloody awful as it has rained on and off now for three days. The section commander of the R.U.R. who got the bullet in the neck has just got the M.M. I relieve Ghari picquet today, and the tents up there are pretty flooded.

April 1st 1939

I COME UNDER FIRE FOR THE FIRST TIME TODAY. I was up at 7022 Picquet which has been shot up before, and on which my platoon was shot up when I was in Nowshera. Well, Barlow's

Crossley armoured cars negotiating Greenwood's Corner.

platoon relieves me at about 12 o'clock so that I can get lunch at Company HQ. I cover his platoon off with two rifle sections lining the nullah bank, and the V.B. on Gaj Ridge. They start to move off the top, and his V.B. gunner stands up to prepare to move from his sangar, on the forward slope of the hill. About eight shots come over him, apparently from the usual place, the graveyard – about 1300 yards from Gaj Ridge. Well, they all get down again, and eventually withdraw two or three at a time, without loss. The MGs open up along with the artillery, and my two rifle sections. During spasmodic shooting, three or four shots whistle over my head on Gaj, and I quickly get down behind the V.B.'s sangar. One hits the bank in front of me, and another by the signaller behind me.

The Royal Ulsters relieved us at Razani, and we marched out without incident, although one of my chapplies was nearly sucked off in the wind on Greenwood's Corner shortcut. The R.U.R. have a wonderful reputation for letting off their rifles. They shoot up anyone who is not wearing a topee or a Gurkha hat. The scouts refused to operate unless given shorts to distinguish them. They shot up the Bombay Grenadiers, who were not having any of it, and replied.

Met Fregard, one of the Ulias *(Unattached list, Indian Army)* for the Garhwal Rifles. The Shaktu incident was apparently as follows: The political agent promised safe conduct to the tribesmen in the cave. They came out and were hustled by the bayonets of the Dogras. Then, thinking that they were to die anyway, they turned on the Dogras, including the C.O., and were all slaughtered. The P.A. had to be hustled out of Waziristan and down to the Plains. Bad luck for him, but his life would have been in danger any longer up here.

April 6th 1939

RAZANI

WHILE OUT HOLDING SHURAGAI, next to Gibraltar, I picked up the jagged base of an exploded Mills grenade on the way home. Letter from Mhairi last night, and Toby is on his way out to Ahomanygen. Manbray is on his way to plant tea in Assam, so I may see him there yet. I hear that Hugh (Colin's elder brother, serving in the RAF) has had his first crash (motor smash) and broke his arm, being now (then, at time of writing) in Cranwell Hospital.

There is a type of crow or shite hawk here that always cries "Hang on, Hang on".

April 11th 1939

RAZANI

A BIT OF SNIPING SOME TWO DAYS AGO on R.P. troops returning to camps, and also during the relief on Conical picquet. On the night of the 9th/10th someone lit a fire in the supply depot. The long row of lorry sheds opposite Bagai's office was burnt down. It must have been sabotage, as the fire started all along the line of sheds simultaneously. Also, several witnesses say that they saw torches flashing inside, and then someone running away. Anyway, it was a damn good fire, though I missed it being in bed, but the next day at about 1.00 pm there was still a flame licking out of a window. Eight or nine vehicles were destroyed, including a few three-ton lorries, reputed to cost Rs 20,000/- each.

April 13th 1939

Razani

A LOT OF THE STAFF COLLEGE ARE UP HERE ON A TOUR. Willie Armstrong and Abbott of 2/13, and Maloney of 1/12 were amongst them. Nelson of 1/8 G.R. is here too, also Seaward, 2/1 G.R. and Harvey-Kelly, 3/10. Beale, Bellamy and one or two others from Harvey-Kelly's school (Bedford Modern) have been killed in recent years, so we wonder how long he will last.

Armstrong says he will see what he can do for me.

A Gurkha in Bakkohi picquet got cut with stone chips, disturbed by a bullet which came into their foxhole from behind him. They were standing to, to help shepherd in R.P. troops.

A lot of shooting yesterday morning, at a couple of picquets or so down the road. Earlier than usual on an R.P. day. Much rain just recently. Brigade commander's inspection today and I handle a sword for the first time in nine months. I have had some of Tundan's and Arora's photographs enlarged to hang on the wall as pictures, and they are not bad at all.[1]

I hear the Staff College contingent got sniped at Dosalli, where they stopped for a demonstration. Willie Armstrong has the lowdown on the Chatfield report. It won't be published, the report that is, only the results thereof. All battalions will gradually be mechanised, except when up on the Frontier, and 16 battalions, including four Gurkha ones, will be given to the War Office. If they don't want them they will be disbanded. Much more likely

'M.G. in action on R.P.' - clearly posed, most likely taken by Tundan or Arora, and the pnt bought by Colin to illustrate his diary.

they will send them to Singapore or Hong Kong to relieve regular British Battalions.

[1] *B R Tundan & Co Ltd and Arora were both professional civilian photographers on the North West frontier, whose images were widely printed for use by British troops.*

April 15th 1939

RAZANI

THE ARTILLERY ARE PRACTISING TODAY, grouping fairly well on their targets, spurs and hilltops. Yesterday we saw Bakshi picquet relieved by 1/8 GR, and they were sniped and there was intermittent sniping for over an hour. The guns lobbed over three or four shells eventually. The only casualty, so the Khasadars told me, was a Kashmiri from the coolie camp who was cutting wood and put his leg in the way of a bullet.

Summer lightning, thunder and rain today. For the past few days there has been a regular hailstorm just after lunch. I go up to Goat picquet today. We send out a Khasadar picquet with a flag to the next ridge. They do a bit of shooting, and then one gabbles in a high-pitched voice to another back home in the Khasadar hut. He then comes and tells me in Pashtu that they have spotted a lashkar moving towards me, and mentions something about machine guns, so I suppose he wants me to get a gun and slaughter the lot. However, the Khasadars let off a few more shots, more come our way, and we get away safely. Holly picquet, next door, has a few shots over them.

An early start today, rising at 5.30 am. I bought Wittington's Smith and Wesson the other day, giving him mine, which he sold to the Doctor, Fowler, for 20 chips.

April 17th 1939

Razani

THE ROYAL ULTERS HAVE BEEN SNIPED a bit at Razani, and when withdrawing from No. 71 they received a volley; two receiving bullets through their fore and aft, and another with one on the puttee.

Had a party in the Club the other night. Nick and I met a couple of Rajputs, had supper and went to the cinema, and put away a good bit of booze. Talks of a column on the 28th – the Munshi[1] says it's rumoured in the bazaar.

Intelligence reports that the 1/8 GR were opposed by about twenty enemy the other day, and says laconically "two enemy hoped hit".

[1] *Secretary/language teacher.*

April 21st 1939

WENT TO THE DUN TODAY, OUT AND HOME BY LORRY, so it wasn't much of a strain. No shooting, but a few shots let off at Toady while withdrawing with 1/8 GR. A gang of about thirty is reported to be lurking around the "RZK area". An R.U.R. was shot in the stomach in Ghari picquet the other day. He was killed, and another got three in the left arm and one in the right. Seems a bit odd to be shot in the stomach behind a breastwork.

I dined with Donald Gordon (2/7) the other night, and took as much as I could hold. I was doing alright until "one for the road" was insisted on, and as I sank that, I could just feel that one more would kill me. The night air wasn't too bracing either, but I made it back safely. We could see Tambre Obo Upper from Dun, which I hadn't noticed the last time I was up there.

April 25th 1939

WENT OUT TO CHAPAO (RAID) on the night of the 21st – two platoons went out, and one lined the wall, standing to. We lay out for about two hours, 8.15-10.15 pm, and saw two jackals in the light of Rifleman Towers' searchlight. Some Gurkhas also went out all night up towards Green Dome, to see if they could catch anything. Went down and talked to some Rajput Indian officers yesterday, but I haven't yet the gift of the gab in Urdu, as have Donald and Mac. I could understand most of what was being said, but could not roll my thoughts out so fluently.

Yesterday I received a bill for Rs 16/- from the "Piffer Mess".[1]

Out collecting detail for a demonstration today, for when the Suffolk's tactical party comes up here. "D" company do three ways of picketing a hill from a column. The first is bloody awful, and we shall all be killed, the second is a bit better, but the chaps have grown "familiar through contempt". The third is the correct way, and no one is killed. An awful lot of bloody rain just now, and a thunderstorm is overhead. I am attached to the Quartermaster for a week, and it's quite an interesting job.

[1] *Mess of the Frontier Force Rifles.*

April 28th 1939

RAZANI

A COUPLE OF DAYS AGO THE LAD who lives between Buckshee and Conical picquets kept up intermittent firing between 1.30 and 4 pm. One shot hit a mule just inside No. 1 gate, and then badly wounded a surveyor Babu. The policeman said he dared not go into his sentry box if it rained, as it wasn't bulletproof.

Yesterday afternoon they saw some snipers lying out in the open, Horseshoe way, and No 2 post sprayed them ineffectively with a V.B. Had a letter from Bill (Bill Robinson, later his best man) today, enjoying himself, but expecting a war in Europe any time, and being rushed to Egypt in case that happens. Went up to Conical on an artillery shoot today. Conical commands a wonderful view, nullahs and reverse slopes innumerable. We controlled the fire by clock code methods, and we were surprisingly accurate. During one lull, an immense boar came ambling out of a clearing and waddled up a nullah out of site. An immense beast he was, and quite out of place up here.

The Rajput Indian officers tried out the skating rink last night and they were damn funny, being old and fairly stout.

Well, today is the day of the supposed column but no reliable news of one yet. Some lads can prove conclusively that there will be one soon, or between such and such dates, with first-hand evidence. Others similarly can prove there will be no column until the so and so'th. I wrote to Colonel Ekin last night to see if I can get any news.

May 1st 1939

Razani

WENT OUT ON R.P., ATTACHED TO 2/7 as the reserve platoon. They do themselves well. They gave me another breakfast. The C.O. brought out his lilo, and they usually take out darts and a pack of cards. 7101 was fired on, going up, and coming down about a hundred shots were let off at it and the HQ. I missed all that. There were supposed to have been three hundred dushmen reported by Alexandra picquet the day before. I go out on rifleman's range today – I put up some tins by the nullah bank and let off my revolver at them. I am surprisingly accurate. A letter from Bill the other day, and his photo in battle dress.

May 6th 1939

Razani

THE RAJPUTS HAVE A COCKTAIL PARTY on the 3rd. I go down at about 8.00 pm and manage to leave at 9. Old Bill Cummyns (3/10) is in good form, and Harvey-Kelly had to be carried back. R.P. next day. Up 7101, very pleasant and a wonderful view from up there. No shooting that day. Next day we have a demonstration rehearsal which isn't too good. I balls up my orders to start with, being accustomed to giving brief directions out on R.P. Yesterday I heard from Colonel Ekin, advising me to write to Major Smyth, the 2nd in command of 2/13 (*2nd Battalion, Frontier Force Rifles, the Indian army unit where CDW eventually transferred*). Col Freeland returns on the 18th this month, so I can but wait and hope. Letter from Reggie Malone. He is due for 3/11 FFR.

May 8th 1939

Razani

D Coy play the C.I.M.H. at ice hockey yesterday. We get ten goals to their five, but a good time is had by all. I have passed the lower Urdu – 127/200 for the oral, and 84/100 for the written. I also have a letter from Niven saying they cannot promise a vacancy, but expect to get one, and will apply to the M.S. for me if I put them down as first choice. Willie Armstrong got onto that for me I think.

May 11th 1939

Razani

On a weapon training cadre under Cpl Clarricoates. Had a spot more ice hockey, and beat up C Coy yesterday. It's just beginning to get hot now, and all the badmashes seem to have left the district. I don't think there has been any shooting for about a fortnight. Drank a few beers in the Club last night, and then saw Donald back to bed. Murray has a wonderful accent, which I could sit and listen to for some time.

May 14th 1939

Razani

Went up to Horse shoe on 12th. It is very pleasant up there, sitting in the sun for eight hours. All quiet save for the buzzing of flies and the odd bee. I try to learn a little Urdu while I am up there. Two horses graze down below. The silence is broken from the ranges under Bakhshi picquet. I take out a short gasht to examine the neighbouring nullahs, and we put up a partridge and a hare. I suddenly realise we have gone a bit too far, and that I should be for the high jump if we caught it. The badmash near Bakhshi puts in a bit of "tachdung-ing". There is a heavy sweet smell from the scrub, and the yellow mossy flowers. Whilst I am having lunch, there is a mighty rushing of wind behind me. On looking round, I see a narrow tornado, about ten yards wide, sweeping up the hillside. One end hits me, and whips off my topee and glasses.

Before the Red Flag appears (to call them in), I spend half an hour watching 7022 cemetery. I see nothing there, but sure enough, later on, the gang opens up. We put a couple of bursts from the V.B. into the cemetery, but I don't believe anyone was really there. The guns put a nice piece of shrapnel just beyond the qabristan (Urdu: cemetery).

District bigwigs are all up here now. I encounter the Intelligence Officer. He says the Brigadier sent 'Bakhshi Joe' a chitthi *(Urdu: epistle or letter, origin of the English word chit)* saying that if he didn't cut it out, he would get his house blown up. 'Bakhshi Joe' has stopped, but another has taken his place. He said that all these chaps wanted was to be such a nuisance to the Sirkar (Urdu: political agent), that we'll say "you ought to be on our side – come and be a Khasadar @ Rs 20/-" All except Ipi, who is honestly thinking of his religion.

Steward of 2/13 is up here on a Mountain warfare course, and is staying in the mess here.

May 17th 1939

RAZANI

YESTERDAY WE HAD OUR FIRST CASUALTY. We are all out watching the final of the British company brigade football. Suddenly bullets come over from Horseshoe way, and land on the pitch. The course soon clears, except for the Brigadier, who sits there as if he didn't know what the matter was. Chaps line the ditch and take cover. Then 'Bakhshi Joe' starts up an enfilade. He hits a man in C Coy in the chest, just coming out of his bungalow. The man dies in hospital shortly afterwards, the doctors saying he never had a chance. We are all damn lucky out there not to cop it, as I see two or three which, with a slight alteration of the Dushman's aim, would have found marks.

An awful lot of flies come out here now. They wake me up between 6.00 am and 7.00 am by buzzing around my head and settling on my face. There is an O.H. *(Old Harrovian, like CDW)* up here, the district ordnance officer, M.W. Scott, from D.I.K. (Dera Ismail Khan). Mickey Wardle gives me the 'lowdown' on Palestine, and from what he says it seems there is some truth in the atrocity stories which the German press gets hold of. He hasn't much of an opinion of the Royal Scots, a pretty bloodthirsty lot apparently.

Went up to Das picquet on the 15th. A very steep climb, one of the steepest I think. On the top, a sangar or two, and a knife edge, overlooking Shimi village. I hold the knife edge, and we get a wonderful view from there.

May 20th 1939

Razani

I GO UP A RIDGE BETWEEN DAS AND DUN again two days ago, part of a brigade scheme for this mountain warfare course. We found a 'sniper's lair' up there. Some rock on the knife edge has been slightly built up to form a sanger covering Dun and the getaway, via Dun picquet. Behind was a tree to give shadow cover, with a few extra branches to help. Suspicious.

I am not on this column on Monday to the Narai. Only fifteen officers are to go, by brigade order. The Ulsters cop it today I believe. They hold No. 72, Knife Edge, M.G., 7 Camp picquet and Khaisora crossing. They had a draft coming out from Palestine. Well, just opposite No. 71 or so, fire was opened on the lorries and on the two sections of M.G. Five men and one British officer were wounded, but it just shows that these chaps can think up a scheme

'Camp rifle inspection'. Image by 'Arora'.

of some sort. They are fired at from Tambre Obo ridge too, which I have picketed many a time.

May 26th 1939

RAZANI

AN ULSTER B.O. – LT DOWLEA MC – got hit by a small piece of stone or bullet in the cavity just below the eye. The column went out on the 22nd and back on the 23rd. A few shots were fired on the way out. About midnight a volley of twenty-five or so fired into camp, but with no effect. Out on a Brigade recce show yesterday on Ghariom road, I got up to near the Postman's Daughter on the ridge up there. The Baluchis (3/10) had quite a battle on the right flank, and I saw the tanks returning from their recce, amid a hail of bullets from quite a short range. One RTC got "splashed" on the ear and a few tanks came home with bullet holes.

The Derby was won by Blue Peter (24th May). It costs me six beers as I divide the runners with Mickey Wardle, eight each, and he gets 1st, 2nd and even 3rd.

Letter from Ma and photo of June's wedding. Also from Pop Jacobs, who is planting nasturtiums on top of his air raid shelter for camouflage, and grows mushrooms inside - so long as the peace lasts, that is. Also heard from Toby, who is with the Camerons in Ahmednagar. I took some very fine pictures of Shini village, and neighbouring hills, from up Das the other day.

An interesting lecture by the Resident on 'policy,' but he didn't really say what the policy is, or why we can't retire to Bannu and build a 'Tegart's Wall.' *(See March 10th)*.

June 1st 1939
Razani

DID A CHAPAO THE OTHER NIGHT. Mickey Wardle sat at Old Reservoir picquet, and I went on to a spur halfway on the wallah between Riflemans' and Landing Ground picquets. There was a bit of a shooting at about 10.30, and one Baluchi was wounded on the perimeter. We just sat there, and listened to the dogs and fellows shouting to each other in the villages. Of course it was bright moonlight, and I could easily have read a book out there. The Coy is now on weapon training, and bloody boring too. Bannu got fired on the other day, with one Indian other ranks being killed. We now have "Whitbread's" beer in the mess, bottled at home, and it's damn good.

June 5th 1939
Razani

TONY WARD ROLLS INTO MY ROOM THE OTHER DAY. He is up from the Devons in Murree to be vetted by the 1/8 GR. We have a few beers in the Club with Nelson and Mickey Wardle. He says Macpherson has gone mad, and is now in a loony bin. I see a very nice trip for £37 on P&O - 2nd class, Bombay, Colombo,

Penang, Singapore, Hong Kong, Shanghai, Kobe, and 10 days in Yokohama. Bombay to Bombay in just under 2 months.

The C.O. turned up to inspect the draft the other day with his topee on back to front, and then capped it all by asking a man "why's your flask on the wrong side?". Then there was the one about Cpl Bunell in Razani, who went up to Reggie Cox and said, "The manager of the Tocky Scouts is here to see you, Sir."

The Gunners gave a pretty wild party on Saturday evening. Many were pierced with darts, hit with billiard balls, and Major Marsden, C.O. of 3/10, was pitched through the window inside. Withington looked a bit battered with his arm in a sling. He tried to jump a sofa I believe, but couldn't see it.

June 9th 1939

Razani

WARD RETURNED. He is only up here for four days, but he seemed to have been a bit shaken by it.

I'm in the ranges under Bakhshi picquet for a few days from 12-4:30 pm. Damn hot down there when there is no wind blowing. The General (Quinan) comes round today; he shakes hands with the officers.

June 12th 1939

Razani

DAVID CAREY'S PLATOON GETS SHOT UP on Dun on R.P. on the 10th. His forward right-hand section is withdrawing from their sangar, and receives a volley from that wooded spar about 40 feet away across the nullah on the right of the Khasadar Hut. One man is killed, having been hit about six or seven times. Two others are wounded (including Farry M.M.), and one who receives a couple but manages to get down and fire his rifle. He claims to have got off five rounds and shot a man whom he saw exposed above his cover to fire. He then was hit again, and has his right arm broken in two places, and one in this arse. Before the shooting, the Khasadars reported forty-eight enemy in sight behind Dun.

Lindsey-Young sent up a couple of platoons onto Das, but they had been withdrawn by the time Dun got the R.T.R. I am in 7101, and see a lot of suspicious movement round the Khasadar flag picquet from Dun. In the end a shell lands a few hundred years below them, which shakes them a bit.

June 13th 1939

Razani

THE TRUE VERSION OF THE DUN AFFAIR is that a couple of shots were fired from Dun and attracted everybody's attention. One section then withdrew from their sangars and down the razorback to Khasadar hut. The enemy then occupied their sangars, and blew up the other section, withdrawing from their sangars. It wasn't far away at the wooded nullah lip.

June 17th 1939

Razani

I TURNED OUT TO PLAY FOOTBALL THE OTHER DAY, and find four teams, including the R.A., in possession of the field. An R.A. officer comes up to me and we sort out the tangle. Then he says, "Are you Hugh D.W?" *(CDW's brother)*. I say, "No," and then it turns out he is Godfrey Pearse, up here after three years in Singapore. I went down Thursday night and had a few beers on him.

There are a lot of dust devils going about just now. We had a lot on the range, and one got into the butts whilst the small figure targets were up, and spun them all around. Bakhshi Joe started up again today, whilst we are on P.T. There seems to be another

'Football against R.A'. Image by the photographer Tundan. Colin is fourth from the right, with a V.

gang around here just now, sniping R.P. troops and being a bloody nuisance.

A platoon on our range covering troops got sniped on Goat yesterday. Shots were hitting their sangars, and they said they saw two of the Dushmen moving in the hillside. And all they did was let them have twenty-one shots from the V.B.

I have brought a pair of soccer boots in the bazaar for Rs14, made at home, and they are a great improvement to my game. We played Pearse and his gunners today, and it was a bloody awful exhibition. They took about 5-1 off us, but their troops know less about the game than I do. They won't kick it, they dribble round and then lose it, and above all, they won't mark their opposite numbers.

Extract from Battalion Orders of yesterday. "All officers below field rank, and all PSMs, will write an essay on the following subject in its relation to the defence of the Empire: "A marked failure to appreciate the factor of TIME on the part of the great democracies is the greatest military danger of the day." It took me the time of two cups of tea before I understood its meaning at all.

The sappers and miners bell has just rung 8, so I must go and drink my troubles away. I'm orderly officer tomorrow again.

June 23rd 1939

Razani

THE BRIGADIER DROVE OUT TO THE NARAI the other day when we were on R.P. He found a bomb there, and so told the Khasadars to destroy it when the troops had left. They had a few shots, and, thinking it a waste of ammunition, brought it in and laid it on the Brigade verandah. The sappers and miners then took it out and blew it up, with the devil of a bang.

A bomb exploded in the R.A. mule lines in Crocus yesterday, wounding two Indian other ranks. I always thought that was a pretty safe spot there. They also shot up the Tower from the heights above, Khasadars or no Khasadars.

I was out covering the range the other day, up a spur near Bakhshi. Suddenly there was a shot, just in front of that picquet, and movement was observed in the bushes. Then a Ghurka appeared, doubling back to Bakhshi picquet, in shorts and vest. In his left hand was a rifle and in his right a long fat hare.

Went out on chapao last night, from 1:30 until 5:30 am. My platoon lined the wall and slept, by No. 4 gate, and Wardle's went out, under Conical near the nullah, to try and catch the dawn snipers, who pot at mules being exercised. They wounded two Indian other ranks in their lats *(latrines)* a couple of days previously, like this. Nothing was seen, of course, save dawn breaking in Waziristan.

I see Geoffrey Holt in 'Picture Post' in the role of "a day in the life of an undergraduate." The cinema here is getting bloody awful films just now. The sort of type you get as runners-up in a provincial cinema, only rather longer.

Donald Gordon has returned from his course, and I met him where he will always be found, in the Club. R.P. tomorrow, and there seems to be a lot of lead flying round here these days.

Tribesmen broke into the British cemetery the other day, hacked trees about, and generally made a nuisance of themselves. I'm told they like the lead in the coffins, to make ammunition. Ipi is reported to be very short of the stuff, but the Dushmen round here seem to have plenty to spare.

June 25th 1939

RAZANI

I WIN THE OFFICERS AND SERGEANTS under thirty cross-country race. The C.O. says he will give Rs10 to the winner, and I just pip Lonsdale for it. I'm up Dun on R.P. yesterday. Practically every picquet was shot up except Das, Dun, Nullah and Goat. 7101 was in action the whole day. About 2000 rounds were fired, and no known enemy casualties. One gunner, an Indian, was wounded on Crocus. You just hold the Khasadar Hut on Dun now. The roof is sandbagged, with a loophole or two, and you sit up there all day.

I sat on a chair in the shade down below, talking to the Khasadars and eating freshly made chapatis. They even shot up Toq. A ricochet from down below bounced over us on Dun. I come running down Dun, just fail to make the Red Flag on a hill, miss it down below in a nullah, and eventually scramble up Crocus to report in. Harvey, the adjutant says, "What are you doing?"

I say, "Reporting in."

"Well," he says, in a nasty voice, "You're taking your time about it, aren't you!"

Willingly I would have shot him, me on my last legs and all. I heard nothing myself, but the air was pretty thick with lead, all down the road. The staff captain reckons the policy is to sit and wait until the locals get fed up with the Badmashes sniping every day, and when they have killed a Khasadar or two, perhaps the Waziris themselves will take action against them.

I had halted, coming back, between a couple of M.G. sections and a V.B. or two, and never have I heard such a noise.

June 29th 1939

OUT ON GAJ YESTERDAY. We leave at 5 am, and back by 2.30 pm. As I was about to withdraw from Ridge, a few shots are let off from a few ridges ahead. I don't know where they go, but Nelson said a few hit the bank on Gaj. It is raining by this time, and the shots sound more like cracks than 'tak-dungs.'

We get in absolutely soaked. A Signals British other ranks got hit in the leg in their canteen the other night. He was rushed to hospital, and the bullet taken out, but he was full of beer and was sick a few times. Since then gangrene has set in, and he has had the leg amputated.

July 4th 1939

HAD LUNCH IN THE MEDICAL MESS ON SUNDAY, at Dunkerton's invitation. A few beers first in the Club, and then we adjourn, Donald as well, at about 2.15. It is just like a breath of bonnie Scotland again, and I discover that Valentine lives in Edinburgh. We then go on to billiards and more beer, and at 4.00 pm I take my leave and go and play soccer. The rest stay until 5.00 pm and later we foregather on the skating rink, even Major James, G.E, as well, for ice hockey.

I take the Higher Urdu exam yesterday, and pass the oral. The second lad in brought out his paper and handed it round, but I was inside, and so missed this bit of "straight from the horse's mouth." The Munshi forecasts that I have passed the written exam as well. I hope so.

A letter from Niven (2/13), that the C.O. says I should go down and visit them in Madras, as it would then be better for all concerned. The C.O. here sends me off to work out the cost, which,

'Rifleman's Tower'

with a warrant and bearer, is Rs150, excluding 5 days' food. Total for the journey I suppose will be about Rs300, a bit much I think.

Lindsey Young then pens a letter to Ellin of 5/13, presumably to ask what it's all about. I personally think that someone else has applied, with strong claims, and they want to have a look at me to see who is the better man. That sounds like 'fall out Dunford Wood.' R.P. tomorrow and today, which they have shot up recently. Still, I am unlucky in these affairs, and I won't even hear a bullet in the air, I bet.

July 7th 1939

RAZANI

R.P. THE OTHER DAY AND TODAY. I win my bet, but it is a very tricky place to hold, and the Khasadars seemed unusually unfriendly. Two shots are fired from somewhere unseen within 300 feet of me, and go whistling over the heads of the rearguard down on the road.

I can't do anything about that though. Forty eight camels are stolen in broad daylight from outside Mirali. I see they have been offered back, 'on payment.' A chit from Brigade comes round saying a great bomb outrage is expected on the Razmak-Bannu road, on the lines of Shahur Tanji I suppose.

I attend an Indian court-martial yesterday and find I can understand all the interpreting. It is at the 2/7 school, and they give us lunch afterwards. I then return and have my first Pashtu hour with old Keroz Khan. Also go to the sergeants mess to watch company billiards with RIASC. Have a few beers and it's a damn good show, in bed by midnight.

Letter from Ma and Uncle George, enclosing Rs 30 for my 21st. Ma's includes messages from Alec and Johnny Graham etc to "Mr Colin, away among those heathens."

July 13th 1939

RAZANI

WE HAVE A BEANO IN THE CORPORAL'S CLUB on the 8th, and Munday confides to me that he was a cracksman before he joined the army. My 21st is on the 9th and I managed to get hold of a few beers in the Club before lunch. I do a bit of Pashti, then a moon about, and finally go down to the skating rink, where there is a party on, as Harry Rickets is going on his leave the day after. I join him and a few sergeants, and then do a bit of alcoholic skating about 9 pm. And so to bed - a letter and Rs30 from Uncle George.

A bomb bounces off Rifleman's Tower the next night, and they put a couple of bursts into some fleeting figures on the 30 feet range. The court-martial is pretty bloody awful, but we are off it for Brigade Day tomorrow.

The 2/7 give us lunch and a few beers, the Munshi reminding me very forcibly of a dog, and I'm sure old Chico Romilly must surely be the 'technical advisor.'

A 'daring holdup' on MS.60 yesterday just below the Narai, and to all intents and purposes unprotected. A Parsot lorry is held up by having its tires shot, four Hindus wounded, shot and stabbed, and about seven kidnapped. At first I thought Attam Khan was on it, as he comes back today, but he rolls in on the Dak Lorry, having had his wife die on him. Two companies of the 1/8 G.R. then did a surprise gasht from Alexandra picquet back along the top. They surprised about thirty enemy on Bare Patch, and I believe gave them a volley at about thirty yards. The enemy made off, apparently more the worse, and one British officer got hit in the arm. That, I fear, will keep them quiet tomorrow.

Colonel Ellin replied to Lindsey Young that I shouldn't spend £25 going to Madras, and he is writing to Freeland. I write to Niven, and say sorry but the C.O. thinks I will be too long away (three weeks). My application form goes in, in sextuplet, to 2/13, 5/13 and 12th[1], so I hope I come out of that alive and with something worthwhile. Wrote to Stephen King Hall for £1 of letters, so I hope it improves my knowledge. Everyone else's essay except mine seems to have come in, so think it must be so bloody awful, it's gone up for review.

Lindsey Young wants to sprinkle Wooded Ridge Tower with pepper, as an anti-sniping measure. The ridicule would be sufficient. He also proposed those old wicker tubes in toy conjuring sets that you put on your finger, and the harder you pull the tighter they become. You have to push into release I think. He would join all Khasadars up in pairs "finger to finger" and have the whole country laughing.

---

[1] *Colin was applying to the 2nd and 5th battalions of the 13th Frontier Force Rifles, and the 12th Frontier Force Rifles.*

July 16th 1939

A SNORTER OF A BRIGADE DAY ON THE 14TH. We went up Zargal Algad to False Narai, Green Dome, and onto Bare Patch. Out from 6.00 am until 6.00 pm. Quite a bit of shooting on the top of that ridge. I had to occupy a sangar position, and whilst rushing towards it through the bushes, about 200 feet away, I saw M.G.s kicking up dust all round it. Peter Withington I believe was screaming his head off, lest I get shot by the M.G.s. Eventually, on another sangar, shooting starts off pretty close judging by the noise. One of the M.G. mule drivers claims to see where it comes from, a bush about 500 feet away. I hold his mule and he opens up with his rifle on it, of course with no apparent result. This is too much for the remaining mule drivers, who hook their reins over the crook of their elbows and start blasting the countryside. I have to put a stop to that, as the mules attempt to bolt.

Eventually reach Bare Patch and find two empty (Dushmen's) rounds. The Ghurkhas apparently surprised the enemy there, drew their kukris and put the enemy to flight, as the tribesmen didn't wait. I also found dried blood, from his arm, which was smashed by a bullet. There was a hell of a lot of it, in a dried pool. Also the cover of his field dressing.

Peter Withington and I were sitting having lunch up there, and a couple of bullets passed over. We reckoned they came from Holly, aimed at another picquet lower down, and were 'overs'. I get lost on the way back and have to carry a rifle home from Bare Patch. A real good wind and rain, sweeping like Tiree. Ian Mitchell is very rude when I reach him, and ask him to point me to D Company HQ. Pretty bloody wet, but enjoyed it on the whole.

Next day we are on covering range on Goat. Corporal Atkinson finds a sentry reading "Spicy Adventure Stories", confiscates it, and when he has read a few, I pass a couple of pleasant hours reading it.

Harrow won at Lords, the first time since 1908, and a free fight took place. How I wish I was there, to bash in a few toppers. R.P. tomorrow, advanced guard – and my heel is bruised through playing ice hockey.

July 18th 1939

RAZANI

A NICE BIT OF SHOOTING YESTERDAY. 7022, Oak, 7021 opposite, and Nik on Das has a bit of shooting too. But the enemy does not hold the forward edge. I sit up to the left of Narai Serai. Suddenly a couple of shots ring out, from a ridge about 300 feet away. One NCO says he sees a man raise himself over the sangar to fire, and that the bullet hits the wall just in front of him. Well, two VBs and MGs open up on this sangar and neighbouring ones, and the most glorious waste of ammunition takes place. Now they start up the other side, below Alexandra picquet, and the Ulsters can be heard having a battle further down the road. Much ado about nothing!

It rains like hell on the way back, a sort of hail, and lucky I have a groundsheet. I pass three reasonable-looking Pathan women. I am shown my report on the attachment, and it's not too bad. I am retiring and inclined to be offhand at first sight, as it were, but apart from that I have the official favour, and "a good knowledge of frontier tactics".

July 21st 1939

RAZANI

THERE'S A REALLY GLORIOUS STORM ON JUST NOW. 2 pm, the usual time for rain, but this time it has got a real good wind at its back. This produces pukka-driven spray such as I haven't seen since I left Tiree. You can see it hurtling along in sort of belts, and the noise on my tin roof, combined with the wind in the eaves and edges, is reminiscent of Island House. Only the wind doesn't whine like it used to. A mighty torrent, breast high in places, rushes down the Nullah under Bakhshi picquet, and catches the range covering troops just as they are being withdrawn. Of course, three fools go and drop their rifles in the waters which whip them away. We all go out in the evening until 7.30 looking for them, and one is found. Two cows were seen, borne capsized past the picquets. Also huge boulders, and as Mitchell said, "I never saw anything like it, it would have been called a cloud burst at home!"

Shades of Tiree – try walking round that corner of the Lodge in January!

R.P. yesterday. I walk out to Gaj and back. The sods don't tell me lunch has arrived, so I would have got none but for Walsh who produced his, and two tins of beer.

July 22nd 1939

Razani

I SPEND ALL MORNING LOOKING FOR THOSE BLOODY RIFLES. I dig up the nullah bed, but no go. Mac has taken over the Company, so I must watch my step, I believe. I give the Khasadars this morning a few "daltah rashas" (come here) and "sahib sara larshaks" which seem to sink home, but they will answer in Urdu. Just as well actually, as I would not be able to understand it if they answered in Pashtu. Dicky Lonsdale tells the RSM (regimental sergeant major) "you know nothing about mountain warfare anyway" as a parting shot after an argument. I reckon he has to apologise, as RSM is insulted to the utmost degree.

Must write to Bill tomorrow, but I suppose I shall be out turning stones for rifles. A boil on my chin, blast it. But it's not going too badly. Last night, whilst beckoning sleep on my bed, I look down and see a glow-worm on the blanket, so I knocked him to the floor and put his glow out, just to be on the safe side, of course.

Doulea of R.U.R. got the MC the other day, down in Razani. The day their draft got shot up, he was MG officer down by Khaisora crossing. His guns had to be unloaded and got into action under fire, and apparently one lad got hit and rolled down into the nullah. Doulea hopped down, under fire, and whipped him up again. He was then hit once more and rolled down the khud, so that Doulea had to bring him up a second time.

July 26th 1939

Razani

THE RIFLES HAVE APPARENTLY BEEN GIVEN UP as lost, and as we are duty battalion, I spend the morning clearing scrub from round the 2/8 lines, from which they snipe the camp at night. Did so yesterday to a chorus of all types of firing from the R.P. troops. Dunkerton says it was the hottest day that they have ever had. 2/7 and 3/10 were out, and they brought in a few Khasadars as prisoners. The ground picquet protecting me opened up, Bakhshi way, at movement they are so good at spotting in head-high scrub at 1300 yards. On the way back I met the Gurkhas going out to picquet Bakhshi range. One of their NCOs salutes me, and twenty minutes later is dead with a bullet between his eyes, next door to Nelson.

About 6 pm, whilst I'm sitting in the Mess reading "Khyber Courtship" by Maud Diner[1], the orderly corporal brings the general 'stand-to' round. Out I double, to find everyone in a flap, and only A & C Coys to stand to. They go out with 1/8 to try and catch some 80-150 enemy located at Gaj. They never succeed of course, but manage to open fire at 600 feet or so, on parties seen making off. They just get in by dark, at about 8.15 pm. Stories come in though. Some lad in the Gurkhas had his company HQ and MG mules in the old Serai at Gaj. Every time he tries to get out the door, a swarm of bullets come over from Oak. He eventually sees a few men taking cover up there, so he lets rip with the MGs, and bugger the Khasadars up there. Three of them, wounded, roll into camp later, complaining bitterly.

Undy's HQ had a signal lamp, pointing outwards towards the forward troops, and this drew fire every time it was used. R.P. troops reckoned they had 1000 rounds fired at them, a couple of hundred in half an hour or so. This is supposed to be given to them by Ipi, and they are blowing it.

A tremendous roar a few nights ago, I never heard it, but they blew up a culvert, though without much effect. Lindsay Young says they are trying to hold up R.P. troops, draw more out of camp, and then hop down and "raid a post, and capture a rifle or two". How the bloody hell, I can't think.

Thursday – tomorrow – and I have to dig a bloody garden.

[1] *In the Cornhill Magazine, July 1939*

July 29th 1939

Razani

R.P. as far as Crocus, to cover a perimeter camp being built there for a scout post. D Coy provides the advance guard, with my platoon on the right. A couple of shots near the tower, but the range was too far and we did nothing about it. Then I am sent up to picquet a hill on Narai side of Toady. It has a village on it, with a large tower. We occupy the hilltop, and put up a bit of cover. In the meantime Toady is being shot up from our front. I and two others are squatting behind a brushwood and barbed wire fence, trying to locate this firing. Suddenly a bullet explodes not two yards in front of us, and we are spattered in stones, and then hear the shot. The other two have had blood drawn by stones or something, and when I get home I pick a bit of lead out of my forearm.

Well, the bullets rain down, they strike our sangar, and I see one chip a piece out of the tower. We nip off in two's, back off the hilltop, and as I am leaping the barbed wire I hear a shot, and the chaps say it whistled over my head. We line the backward slopes, and one man says he saw a rifle barrel poke out of the tower and fire at us. I don't believe it, as if this had been so he could hardly have missed at 50 feet. Still, we put a few shots into the tower. One man has left his pack and mug behind that exposed sangar. He says it's not worth risking a life to get it. Then like a fool (I must have been wishing to show off) I hop the wire and rush out there and get it. As I get to the sangar he takes a shot at me and I apparently groan and take cover, as Pierce comes charging over with putties flying shouting "Are ye hit sir, are ye hit?

He helps me up and we run back. I drop my stick and pointer staff, I pick up the pointer but he urges me not to go back for the stick, so it is "abandoned to the enemy". I try to get a man from the village to get it, but they are all so snug I cannot make contact with anyone. They pot us from time to time and we eventually retire, by dribbling off, and as the last sections go, there comes two parting presents, the first ones I hear that whine.

We get back to Crocus, and I am sent on to a spur of Toady to cover it down. Then I discover I left my pipe and field glasses up on that picquet too. Rearguard home, and when just above 70 milestone nullah, Mike Wardle's platoon gets shot at, doing rearguard over Pink hills. Private Tew gets hit in the calf. I locate the firing, and open up with V.B., and then take two sections up under cover of Pink hills to see if I can help. Can't help, so return. We continue to withdraw under a few bullets, and then make Gaj. Here Micky and I cover eighteen troops back from the ridge in front, as they retreat through us. They get over, and are nipping across the flat behind Gaj, when there is 'crack!' – they all fall to the ground and Private Newberry is hit in the arm. Chaps shout for stretcher bearers "This way! That! Medic wanted!" etc. So I leave the shelter of the Gaj Khasadar post and nip down to him. His arm is already bandaged, but he is almost 'out' with the shock and pain so Smith, an NCO, and I hustle him along to a hole by the road. There is a 'crack' and a spurt just as we get there but we make it safely. I then run back up Gaj, and an armoured car comes and takes him away. We are all then pinned to Gaj – three platoons - by two or three men! I thought there was only one man, as we never heard two shots one after the other. All three VBs open up, and two of my men spend the next half hour taking periodic pots at the top of 7022, where of course they "see" movement.

The Red Flag is nearly in the barracks, but Mac signals back and they send out MG and artillery to extricate us. The platoon on the ground gets off creepy crawly Indian fashion by twos and threes, and after half an hour's shooting I get the RTR (military parlance 'ready to return'). Off by sections and run like hell down to the road where there is cover. Mickey Wardle doesn't get the order (he is on the 7022 end) and is left behind for twenty minutes as his signaller is "taking cover". He gets the shock of his life when he finds that I have left him there alone, but that's Mac's fault. There must surely be questions asked as to why Mickey was doing rearguard out as far as Pink Hills. Mac's to blame for that.

They reckon they inflicted seven or eight casualties on that evening show the other day. Last Thursday I am sent on Brigade garden fatigue (labour). There the Sanitary Inspector shows me the Brigade letter that says the fatigue will not be done Thursdays and Sundays. Dick Harvey of course never saw the letter. Blast his eyes.

July 31st 1939

RAZANI

I FIND TWO MORE PIECES OF LEAD, on my chest and forearm, making three in all. I hear all the guns are going to open up at 7.00 pm tonight, suddenly, on the Sidar Alghad, at a range of 4500 feet. It sounds rather grotesque. R.P. tomorrow, but I don't expect I shall even smell a bullet.

August 4th 1939

THE GUNS NEVER OPEN UP. It was that gunner Langford, with the head like a latrine bucket, who started it.

I smelt a couple of bullets on the R.P. yesterday. A new system of Company areas and local gashts was tried. Tanks cooperated, and it all seemed fairly successful. One man got his rifle hit on the fore end on Crocus.

I run 11/20 in the inter-company mile team race. It nearly kills me. Clarke has returned from an attachment to the RAF in Peshawar. That madman P.M. Bond is there, presumably on a short service commission. Intelligence reports three killed and eight wounded on the 25th, mostly during the evening sortie

August 7th 1939

THE 5/11 WENT OUT AT MIDNIGHT the other night and lay up round Green Dome and Bare Patch. Then 3 Bn Brigade went out the next morning, but no one was caught. One British other ranks shot in the stomach out on R.P., not a pleasant wound I believe. The sergeants came into the Mess for tea and tennis at 5.00 pm. After tea comes beer, and they left at 8.45 after much darts and billiards. A 'tippet' school started, but the RSM breaks it up by saying it's time to push off. R.P. at Dun tomorrow.

A good cartoon in C&M – an armoured car on a broken bridge, signed 'To Waziristan', with its nose in the river, and the tank wallah sitting on the roof with his head in his hands and a cigarette dangling from his lips. A lot of wild-looking tribesmen are rushing down to get him, firing their rifles in the air and waving swords. He says "And they call this peaceful penetration".

August 11th 1939

UP DUN THE OTHER DAY, BUT NO SHOOTING. I chat with the locals in Pashtu and Urdu fairly successfully. Colonel May was shot in his car yesterday evening, outside Bannu on the Mari Indus road. He dined here about ten days ago, with District HQ staff. The Frenchman is staying with us now and Major Callander (2nd in command of the Leicesters) is very amusing about him. A French Canadian comes into the Mess last guest night, and gets as pissed as an owl – and aggressive too.

A letter from Johnny Benbow, who reckons on going to 4/15 in Landi Kotal. I hear from Tony Ward, and under section 143(1) I get the Indian Army allowance from the date of passing Higher Urdu. Therefore on September's pay bill I ought to collect just under 800 chips.

August 13th 1939

RAZANI

DID ADVANCE GUARD TO NARAI and sat on Duncan's picquet. A bit of sniping from the slopes behind Toady, and the Scouts did a gasht in the hills west of Pink Hills. They had a good battle, and most of the day we saw shells bursting over there. I went up to Alexandra picquet in a staff car and had a beer with Donald Gordon. Inside it looks as though it might have stepped out of some film of the frontier, or Beau Geste. A wooden, railed platform all round the top of the wall, for stand-to, gives this impression. A very interesting log book is shown me, with some bloody funny entries in it. The Scouts did a gasht up that way, and were fired on. Some of the garrison are reputed to have heard them say "Don't shoot, we are Scouts", and the shooting stopped.

The Sappers blew up a bomb on the road a couple of furlongs from the Narai, and I see half a culvert that has been blown in, a night or two previously. I also saw some fragments of this bomb, which certainly looked tough enough. They reckon Alex is the highest permanent picquet in the Empire – but I don't know about that.

The Brigadier is reputed to have said that Ipi (now in Khame, so why the hell don't they blow him out of it) is sending up a gun or two to the Razmak front. It is almost a proscribed area up here now, as all the locals have orders to stay indoors on R.P. days, so that anyone out, if not a Khasadar, is liable to get shot. Though I'll be damned if I have ever seen a man yet who might be enemy. You hear the shot, or the bullet arrives, and God bless the Duke where it comes from.

A letter from Clapham today. *(Where his brother Hugh's new wife lived, pregnant with their first child).*

This munshi, Feroz Khan, is very bad mannered. Whilst your attention is fixed on "Hagha Dagha" *(Pashtu: this and that)* or "Khwab o'khial", or whatever it be, he slides a hand up his shirt, rummages about for a little, as though searching for tin tacks in the bottom of a bed, and then produces a long white hair, plucked from the shrubbery on his chest. He then holds it and contemplates it, almost regretfully, finally depositing it on your best Persian carpet. He cast a great many with Mickey Wardle but I, duly warned, used to watch him carefully when he was fiddling about, trying to unbutton his shirt, and stare so hard that he gave it up. Alas, the other day I looked up from the book and saw his hand come out like a snake from his bosom, and the deed was done. When he had gone, there shone a long, thin white hair on the floor.

Corporal Farry has the Military Medal for his effort on Dun on April 10th. He was badly wounded, but continued to fire back, and I reckon he killed the leader of the gang. Some say he was hit in the right shoulder and then turned over and fired from his left shoulder, but I wouldn't know about that. The 2/7 are hanging their shield on August 23rd, and Donald expects to come down from Alex for that. I must get into training as there are only ten days left.

August 15th 1939

Razani

HAD AN INTER-COY FOOTBALL GAME on Sunderland ground today. Some time before halftime, the bullets started to come over, about half a dozen I should think, and a few landed on the pitch. We all ran like bloody cheetahs and got off with no casualties. No 2 post V.B. opened up on a sangar on Horseshoe ridge, where they were supposed to be.

The whole Brigade is going out tonight. Three battalions at 24h00 to surround the villages opposite Dun, on the other side of the road, Mir Khan Khel and Spanam Khel. Anyone out of doors to be treated as enemy. We go out at 02h00 and picquet up to Toady to cover the troops coming home. I have Toady, and need to get up at 01h15.

August 17th 1939

Razani

I MANAGE TO GET TO BED AT 10.30 PM after listening to Mac's detail. However, what with Clarke's wireless, and sort of thinking of the morrow, I get no sleep, and get up at 1.00 am to a cup of tea and half a dozen biscuits. Well, we set off at about 2.00 am and take about half an hour to cross the aerodrome and get onto the road. From there it's all Plain, on the road all the way, and I don't care a damn if they do hear the noise we make with our boots, and open up.

I am sent on to Crocus where I halt, at about 4am, and wait for dawn. I hear two lads come shuffling down the road, so I hop out

The 'post gun' at Razani, fired at dusk to alert the patrols to return to camp.

with my revolver and hold them up. One complains in English that they are Baluchis, and looking for transport. At first light I send up a Khasadar, though he seems goofy and unable to understand my pashtu, and then we follow him onto Toady. The very devil of a noise starts on the other side, and goes on the whole day. There is a bit of shooting on the 7101 side, and we open up from the roof with the V.B. On coming off, we open up (Corporal Webb and his five rounds rapid) to keep their heads down, but I don't think they were really firing at us.

A couple come over on the way home, but I get in at 1.00 pm, shave, bathe, tiffin and am in bed at 2.00 pm to sleep like a snapdragon until 7.00 pm. Up at 7.30, bathe, and Pearse comes in. Afterwards over beer everyone discusses the day's operation.

The Scouts rounded up 58, who are in a "cage" down by the Treasury, guarded by 5/11 and surrounded by a speculative audience of all races. Some got away into the hills, and shot up picquets at 200 feet. A few got in between the outer and inner picquets of 2/1. They shot up the inner ones and then gathered their cloaks and themselves and went into a huddle, for a council of war. One of the outer picquets then got them in the rear with a VB.

2/1 met a party suddenly round a nullah, at ten yards range, and claim to have shot five out of seven of them. 58 prisoners were taken out of the village, and nine enemy estimated killed, but only three bodies recovered to date, and one rifle. The tanks fired an immense quantity of ammunition, and one gurkha got hit in the arse and the other in the knee, the bullet travelling up to near his ribs. All the village dogs started off about half an hour before dawn, and I heard cocks crowing as well. The prisoners were mostly locals from those two villages, with a few badmashes as well, and are to be interrogated about that hold-up below the narai on July 12th.

August 18th 1939

Razani

Road open today, and the 6-inchers open up from camp during lunchtime. At least everyone says they are 6 inchers. Had a meeting on the Roller Skating Hockey last night, down in the rink, and I hope to get the show starting sometime next week.

The Intelligence Reports say that Toady was continually shot up on 16th. The first I knew of it. Had arranged to continue that football match today, which was broken up by snipers on 15th, but the troops refuse to play, blast their cowardly souls. Still, it's just as well to give it a rest I suppose. Lt Col May had powder marks on his body and had been shot with a shotgun. A log was placed across the road, but he must have had his revolver unloaded, or under the seat I think, or he would not have been shot at such close range.

Mickey Wardle came off 7101 too soon the other day, owing to the signaller's mistake. Mac, of course, says "When the signaller said to you RTR, did you ask him 'Did HQ say to you No 7 picquet RTR?'" Like hell he did! Mac has never been up a picquet, the bloody fool. God help the Coy on a column with him as OC.

August 19th 1939

It was the post guns yesterday afternoon, but at about 7.30 pm the 6-inchers went out onto the aerodrome and opened up. They took some time, as they forgot the rangefinder, and had to send back for it. Some locals apparently came in and said that parties of hostiles were in their area, and would we open up? Anyway, they had two targets, and put four six-inch shells on each, and they made some noise too. The RA have to stand-to most of the time to cover the Tochi Scouts camp on Crocus.

August 22nd 1939

We were playing a game of Ice Hockey with the C.I.M.H. (military hospital) when at about half time the referee blew the whistle to halt play and a police corporal came and saluted and said "All Leicesters to return to barracks, sir!" That starts another night show, from which half a dozen chaps do not return. We are on the right flank, guarding the Green Dome area, 2/1 G.R. are left flank guard, and 5/11 and 3/10 are going via Bare Patch to surround a gang at Bandiza, together with the Scouts. I hop into bed from 10 to 11 pm and then we set out at midnight. I am to picquet Conical, the rest of Coy to picquet Cliff. We pass a drunken gunner in the cells shouting "I want to see a medical officer – I want to see etc etc" like a gramophone record that has stuck on one groove.

I am in front with Callander (2nd in command of the Leicesters) and Lonsdale for the night march, and it's damn funny. Callander with stick out, searching for wire or nullahs, and I hop gaily down the nullahs, which I can see, and get warned off for going too fast. I lead off, and we go up by the butts, hoping to strike a path for the M.G. mules. We do, and lose it twice, but arrive under the tower at 1.30 pm. We halt there until dawn, and then take up positions on the ridge. Bloody cold till dawn, the sweat of climbing the hill freezing in my shirt. I manage to get a groundsheet, but it's still bloody! We get tea from the tower and a charpoy, onto which some good Sikh brings out some bedding. There we stay until 7 pm.

A lot of shooting, Bare Patch way, and I see a hut go up on Horseshoe. The main body gets up OK, but Callander is told by villagers below Prospect Corner to be careful, as the place is crawling with enemy. He has to lead the whole Battalion expecting a volley at any minute.

"C" Coy have a picquet to the right of Postman's Daughter. It's on a forward slope, with a ridge in front of it, so I understand. A party of twelve armed men is seen on the road. It's not an R.P. day, so they cannot be fired on. The Khasadars shout "who are you?" and they nip off the road into the bushes. They could have been wiped out. C Coy's picquet is then fired on, the forward section being obliterated, and the remainder of the section running back. Then, under cover from the overlooking ridge, a knife party comes up, and two bodies and rifles are lost. What happens then I don't know, but eventually Nick goes forward with three men to look for the bodies. He sees eight dushmen at fifty yards running off, and after some trouble, gets out his revolver and gets off three rounds at them without success. The bodies are not found, though several attempts are made.

A lot of gallant deeds are done in rescuing chaps lying out in the open, and Walsh (R.A). is hit in the arm at 2 pm. He carries on directing the guns until 7 pm, so I expect he will collect an M.C. Six men are killed and six wounded, from C Coy and the M.G. section. Hundreds of guns open up from camp, and a short one lands on Postman's Daughter. A couple of snipers are under here on my side, but they don't do much damage. An aeroplane arrives, and bombs and machine guns enemy, as C Coy put out a 'T' – Flight Lt Gilbert gets a DFC for this. Two companies from 2/8

G.R. arrive on Conical from camp and send two picquets onto Prospect Corner Ridge. An ambulance arrives for the bodies, goes round the bottom corner by Prospect Corner, and is fired on from Skyline Ridge. I open up with M.G.s but it seems pretty useless so we knock off. The bodies can be seen coming down the hill on stretchers, the dead covered with a groundsheet, and the living with their heads left out. The aeroplane covers the Battalion down, ridge by ridge. I get R.T.R. about seven, and we are back by 7.30. Everyone lines the road to see us come in – a funny sight.

Khasadars later find the equipment of one body, less rifle, bayonet and ammunition, on Green Dome, and send it home.

Thirteen enemy are killed, including Khan Gul, one of Ipi's commissioned officers. The Brigade must have had twenty casualties. It seems the scheme was a balls-up. The Scouts were two hours late, and only half the village was surrounded. The Brigadier must have been so elated by his first night operation, and has taken a backhander from the enemy on this one. I wish I had been up on Postman's Daughter. I never smelt a bullet even. That makes the score eight killed, and ten wounded. The retreat is followed up with shooting all night long, near Rifleman's Tower. A raid is expected in Bannu just now. Officers go about in pairs, after dark, and armed.

August 25th 1939

Razani

THE TWO BODIES BROUGHT IN BY KHASADARS are untouched by mutilation. Four rifles have been lost, and eight enemy are known to have been killed, and Gagu's brother seriously wounded. The political administrator, Major Bacon, says there were four hundred enemy in that area that day, so we were damned lucky.

Rumour now has it that Ipi is out to get a British officer of this regiment in revenge for Khan Gul. I don't know about this, but I expect it will become rather dangerous round here during the next fortnight.

Signs of a war in Europe. All British citizens have been ordered to leave Germany, which I reckon is a bad sign. All officers passing through Bannu, by road or rail, have to report to Bannu Brigade, so a notice in the Club says. All leave stopped, in and ex-India.

August 30th 1939

Razani

DID ADVANCE GUARD TO CROCUS the other day. Nick on Pink Hills observed three men come out of a house and sit sunning themselves. He immediately opened up with his V.B., under the "Proscription Act", and saw one fall, which pleased him greatly. I was nearby, with Mickey, and whilst on Crocus, in the rain, we saw some chaps on the road about 1200 feet back who were coming out of a village. Also a man and a woman walked across Nullah picquet. We discuss whether to open up or not. I maintain that the road is closed behind us, and that therefore we have no excuse to murder them. Eventually Wardle compromises by taking a shot with a rifle at the woman on Nullah at about 900 feet and missing her. The adjutant later says that my opinion was correct, but that if they are observed armed, then by all means open fire.

Mickey, Pat Burder and myself bought a bottle of whiskey and went down to call on Walshe in hospital. Nick and Godfrey Pearse then arrived with another bottle, and we had a party. I had four stengahs (whiskey and soda over ice) and found that that was quite sufficient – "One more and I die".

Intelligence reports say that Ipi has gone into conference, and intends to make big trouble in ten or fifteen days time (about Sept 5th). I hope so, as I have got the job of A.P.M. *(Assistant provost marshal)* in this month's Razcol, through knowing Urdu, and Burder, a Company commander. A letter from Bill, on two months leave at home, and Daphne.

September 3rd 1939

Razani

WENT AND DINED WITH PEARSE IN THE R.A. MESS. The nicest mess in Razmak. Captain Findlay (O.H.) with one arm was there. On his artificial arm he had a hand which he could unscrew and, in its place, insert a hammer and screw it up. Damn funny it looked. Champagne, madeira, white ladys and beer, so I was bloody lucky to be in bed by 1am. I think Godfrey thought I was a bit of a wet going off so soon, but what of it!? Shaw, new Ulia, said that, at R.M.C. (Sandhurst), when French reserve officers came down to inspect, during one interminable salute one laddie took his right hand down and surreptitiously slipped up his left in its place, to give it a rest – Shayad! (Urdu: perhaps).

War about to start any minute now, so I am putting in a bit of packing, in case I get ordered to the "something-th" regiment by "next R.P. day". I want to sell those Persian carpets, but no one in the bazaar will take them. I have now given them to a Bagai agent, who is also a licensed government auctioneer.

Blimey seems to be on the wagon (almost) after his leave in Kashmir. I remember one guest night how he had to help his port glass up to his mouth with his left hand, during toasting the King, as the other was shaking so much that it couldn't make it.

War declared today – celebrated in true fashion.

September 5th 1939

Razani

CAME BACK FROM FOOTBALL ABOUT 4.30 PM on Sunday and we could just hear Chamberlain saying that a state of war existed with Germany. This was on Ian Mitchell's wireless, and we had to put our heads almost up to the machine to hear. Went into the Sergeants Mess at about 10.00 pm – Jack Greasly, Jackson, Burder, Miller,

Wardle and self. Pat Miller had to be taken back at about 10.15 pm, being too full of champagne, which he had sunk at dinner. Mickey took him, and apart from falling in a drain on the way, he arrived safely. Pat Burder very drunk, and slurring his words. The RSM in great form, and made a speech or two as did everyone else. I rendered "a portly Roman Senator", which shook some of them.

Yesterday was the 2/7 shield hanging party. I had a beer or two, and some lime juice, and then left the Club at about 9.00 pm, as was feeling a bit weak in the legs after football and the night before in the Sergeants Mess.

Mickey Wardle was brought home about 11.00 pm, having passed out cold when he got outside the Club. His door was shut, so Clive Pearson (1/12) broke through his fly proof window to open up. He then woke up in the morning feeling on top of his form, but with a bed full of sickness beside him. What a lad!

News yesterday morning of "Athenia" being torpedoed off Scotland. In about two hours the rumour was round it had been torpedoed with the Royal Scots on board. Never understood how it got like that!

September 11th 1939

Razani

POSTINGS ARE OUT, and I have the 2/13 *(2nd battalion, 13 Frontier Force Rifles)*. The awards also received for the Bodhari Sar show. Walshe has an M.C., Sgt Blake a DSM – he led search parties out several times looking for the bodies, and L/Cpl Rawson an M.M. He is a machine-gunner, but I don't quite know what he did. These are immediate awards, and others may have been sent home and recommended.

Got shot up on the range for the first time in this "war". I had been scoring in butts, and was returning along the Maidan, outside Coolie Camp, when a dushman between Bump and Bakhshi opened up. He had the range too long, and they sang over our heads well out of reach. I was due to bring down the covering troops, and am halfway through this operation, when of course Mac needs to get out of bed and do it himself, damn it.

A mixed platoon of "D" Company is on R.P. tomorrow, commanded by Burder. I go to the Adjutant and say that it is my platoon and what a disgrace the whole show is. He says yes, and you command it. So I have wangled a last R.P. tomorrow, and here's hoping, though as Ossy is commanding the detachment, I doubt they will allow us anywhere dangerous if it can be helped.

Holly tomorrow, the only picquet I have never been up, so that means a peaceful day, as nothing can ever happen up there.

September 14th 1939

RAZANI

I GO UP OAK EVENTUALLY. There is a bit of shooting on several picquets. Some sniping comes from the sangar, Bare Patch way, just above me, however they fire on everyone but us. Two shells arrive up there, so I put in two bursts of V.B. fire to sort of keep the pot boiling. This has the desired effect, and no more shooting from up there. "C" company on Horseshoe were shot up, Private Woodward being killed, and one other getting hit in the arse. I don't believe these buckshot stories. It's broken bullets or stones.

That night Pat Miller, Nick, and myself give a party in the Club lounge. We invite the Mess, Purcell, Nelson, Pearse, Gordon, Dunkerton, Valentine, Seaward, Wellwood and Gillan. A very successful party. The first lad comes about 7.20 pm and then we walk out on Gordon and Wellwood at 10 pm. Everyone said it was very original, and that Razmak had never seen the like before.

Yesterday I ran the bloody mile and got 11/20. Also a sore throat from coughing so much when I got back. Nick and I had drinks with Walter Purcell, and were then dined out. I reckon I consumed about 2 1/2 bottles of beer, two gins, two madeiras, a whisky and a sherry, and didn't turn a hair. Got to bed at 12.30

pm and up at 6 am with "dawn patrol". A good party last night. Col. Weld was there and I made his acquaintance officially. I hear a platoon of scouts met a hundred dushmen on Bare Patch the other day, and that the enemy told them to "bugger off, we don't fire at you" – and they did too!

Part 2

2nd Battalion
13th Frontier Force Rifles

Madras / Abbottabad

September 26th 1939

MADRAS

NOW IN MADRAS. Before leaving Razani, was given a farewell party in the Sergeants Mess – Miller made his same speech again, and when he sat down, CSM Blackwell said "I wish I had your command of English, sir." RSM then invited me to get up and beat it, which I believe I did with one or two cracks against the CSM of "D" company.

On Friday I was kept on the range until 2 pm, and that evening I had drinks with Colonel Weld in the District Mess. We had a pretty awful trip to Bannu, each with the front seat in an empty Bagai lorry, and stopped at the Narai to say goodbye to those present at Battalion HQ. Met a gunner, Tom Christopher (81 Field Artillery), and Donald Gordon at the rest camp, and had a swim, and saw the flick on the club lawn, very pleasant, as you sipped beer at the same time. It was there I saw the first woman for six months, since I saw a brace in Kohat.

Got to Mari Indus the next day safely, having said goodbye to Nick on the platform. We filled the Heatstroke Express (the train) with ice and were damn cool, it all dripping out of the door at the halts. Reached Rawalpindi early the next morning, and Christopher had us up to the gunner's mess for the day. I read all the "Times"s and bought a 10/- thermos canteen, which has been very useful since. In Bannu I found my cigarette case was missing, so I wrote to Micky Wardle to look for it, but I think I have seen the last of it. Gora Miller was left at Meerut, and I changed at Delhi. The restaurant Babu walked me round the fort, about five miles, and then I met Donald and a lad in 2/8 Gurkhas and we went to Maiden's Hotel. We drank beer and gin, and watched some beauties who were there, including a French girl. I then left that afternoon and reached Madras two days later at 1800hrs. In Itarsi was a train load of Germans, bound for an internment camp and guarded by armed policemen at every carriage door. The captain in charge said he had one carriage of Nazis and one of Jews and they wouldn't look at each other, neither would the Jews drink Becks Beers.

Palmer met me in Madras, and we went out to the Mount in the regimental bus. I met Symonds there, and next morning Niven and C/O Smythe, Freeland being in the Fort at Madras, commanding the station. Drinks at Jimmy Smythe's and the Niven's houses. Madras is nine miles away, but John Palmer and I went in the other night for a drink at the Connemara to meet a girl of his, and then to the flicks afterwards. We met the girl – a Mrs Honor Ransome (hubby Royal Indian Navy) – in her room, and so did five other men, including one Freddie Holmes (Flt/Lt DFC), and a lad by the name of Mac. They all danced with Honor, and then Jo and I went to the cinema with Mac. After that we returned to his room in the Connemara, and drank beer and sandwiches and talked. I got to bed at 0130 and up again at 0530 on company training by Black Rocks.

John's girl Honor then came out here last night for booze with one May Green, wife of Lt Green RIN, as chaperone. John has a large notice 'Ladies' above the door of his ghugle khana *(dining room)*, and they use it, too! They are both now coming to dinner here tonight, in the "Ladies Room". So God help us – or me, as John won't need it.

LIST OF OFFICERS, 2ND BN, 13TH FRONTIER FORCE RIFLES

Lt Col Freeland R.A.B. MC Command Madras
Major Smyth J. Present C.O.
Major Goode R.L. GSO India Office, London
Major Gilbert C. on leave
Major Morris C.F. DSO on leave
Major Woods D.L.O. OBE S.W. Scouts
Capt Nash J.H.E. Jhansi Brigade H/Q
Capt Abbott B.E. Staff College

Capt Armstrong W.J. Staff College
Capt Keen P.J. Political
Capt Wainwright V.L.M. MC T.B.
Lt Niven R.W. Present Adjutant
Lt Elsmie R. T.B.
Lt Steward R. Commanding Trichinopoly
Lt France M.H.C. on leave
Lt Beale G.F.A. on leave
Lt Symonds R.H.B. present
R/Lt Palmer J.B. asst QM present

October 2nd 1939

MADRAS

THAT PARTY WITH THE HARRIDANS went off all right. They were only two hours late in arriving, and I had to look after the heavyweight May for many an hour, whilst John went about his business with Honor. Yesterday went out after snipe with Niven. Left here at 5.00 am with a shikhari[1], and no one spoke Tamil, so it was rather difficult.

Eventually we reached the place, and for three hours we waded through paddy fields. Some were so full of water that the snipe would need to swim to get anywhere but we saw three. Niven killed one and I missed one, after having opened up on a sandpiper by mistake (and missed him). Romany kite, Kingfisher, Paddybird, Bee eater and Blue Jay seen for the first time.

Yesterday afternoon went to Gordon Woodroffe's factory sports as some of Sikh Coy were competing. Met a lad by the name of Cole, who is one of the "Key-men of industry" here. He taught me the one word of Tamil essential to know, "Poida", meaning "Get the hell out of it". No mail from home since the war (started), and only one from Grindlays, forwarded from Razmak.

[1] *Guide/hunter.*

October 8th 1939

MADRAS

WORK, TENNIS, FOOTBALL AND BOOZE. Maitland, France, Gilbert and Morris returned from leave, having doubled half the Atlantic in a convoy and been attacked by submarines in the Mediterranean. A partridge drive is arranged for today, but the shikhari never turned up last night, so Ray cancelled it.

Did a Battalion scheme yesterday. I took two Indian officers out the day before, and showed them the ground, and gave them orders. Mahan Shand of course altered it a good bit, and as I not fluent in the language he gets away with it. I can't sell these damn carpets. The bloody furniture wallah won't come and won't cooperate. (Sent them to Hugh as a wedding present!)

October 14th 1939

MADRAS

ON THURSDAY WENT IN TO WATCH the Wiltshire's retreat, in the fort, had supper, and watched our Khatlak dance, which was laid on in the fort for the benefit of the troops. First one I ever saw, and it was good, though the ground was too hard for hurling themselves about, and in mixed company it was quite clean. After that we went to Connemara, John, Maitland France and self. I had one dance with Mrs Green, not being invited to the other party, but she had an awful, grim man in the navy department.

So I go up to Maitland who is sitting talking to a girl and I say "May I steal you away?" to the girl (not France), and Maitland introduces me and I keep her for the rest of the evening. One Celia Mockett, who's father is a judge here. One other gent asks her for a dance but apart from that, I do very well. A few catty remarks made on the way home.

I wonder if I shall see this war. The Koikhais think we shall go to Wana, and if so I reckon we shall be forgotten and left to rot – unless the Mashouds should decide to try their luck again. We never get any gossip here, as in Razmak, as apart from us and the Wilts (1st Battalion, The Wiltshire Regiment) in Madras, there are no other regulars. I read the Madras Mail in the mornings after breakfast, and the pictures of troops off to, and in, France that I see make me grumble over my lot for the rest of the morning. How long we stay here I don't know but John (QM), was asked yesterday by the powers above if we had accommodation for an imposing list of M.T. But then we are not equipped for war in Europe, and Congress are trying to blackmail London to give them Dominion status before India helps in the war.

Bought a 17/6d air gun – a Tell – for 38 rupees here, at Orr's – the bloody shark – for shooting tree rats. Good sport. 12 bore cartridges are 17/-, though last time I enquired before the war they were 12/- / 13/-, and they are surely the same stock, so it is only profiteering.

A guest night with the Wiltshires tonight, so I suppose I shall get no sleep, as I hope to go out shooting tomorrow at the crack o'dawn. No letters since the war, and I should like to see an English paper again. Must do something about these carpets.

I have the bloody job of learning Indian Officers' and keymen's jobs, being closely questioned every morning by Ray Niven in the orderly room.

October 18th 1939

Madras

THE WILTS CAME TO A GUEST NIGHT LAST SATURDAY. Met one Jos Redman, who seemed to get a bit pissed towards the end. After dinner the bloods played 'Crown and Anchor' (a dice game) which I got from Spencer's – seemed to go down very well. Next day, went out shooting with Niven. Not too good, as I got to bed after the guest night at 2am, and up again at 5. Missed a partridge right overhead, God knows why, except that the gun does not fit. We also saw, and walked up to, about eight of what the shikhari called prairie snipe (Golden plover) – got off two shots and missed them as well.

I get rather depressed sometimes over this war, after having read the papers, but I'm damned if I see how I am to get near it – let alone to France. God help me if we go to Wana, as we will be forgotten there, so God help us again.

October 21st 1939
MADRAS

THERE ARE ONE OR TWO FUNNY CHAPS in the Wilts detachment up here. There is a Major Bearen, with a damn pretty wife, who is the "compleat tennis rabbit". One Major Ludford, known as Babe, whose wife has a mind like a lavatory – their children's nurse is one Lulu, who is courted by the troops. 'Doc' Cunningham and Robbins, with little Audrey, and a madman called 'Dopey' Hamilton. The Ludfords had passed some remarks about Dopey at their table one day, and later on Ludford took one of his small daughters across to the PRI's store. He was there in conversation with a CQMS when Hamilton happened to go past. Daughter turns round and says "Look Daddy – there's that wet officer again."

Must get down to a bit of work for the Retention exam – all the organisation and interior workings of the Battalion.

October 27th 1939
MADRAS

BEALE RETURNED FROM LEAVE LATE, not having received his recall telegram. John, he and I spent last Saturday in the Connemara after dinner, in observation. A letter from Ma, announcing Hugh's marriage to Peggy Farlow. Wrote to Hugh and Uncle Bill. I am informed I go to S.A.S. Sangor, January 25th - March 10th, and must pass the Retention exam before so doing – what fun.

Observed a very good sunset last Sunday from Elliot's beach, where I was bathing. We have done a bit of riding lately, towards the Adyar, though unfortunately over the golf course. British officers plus Indian officers vs Wilts Officers and sergeants of the detachment up here.

October 31st 1939

Madras

WERE BEATEN IN THE ABOVE MATCH 1-2. That night Jerry Beale, John and I went to the cinema, and then to the Connemara. We got in without paying Rs 2/- and had a few drinks and sat in observation. Doreen Hope, Lady, was there, she's known locally as the Red Streak. But very nice all the same despite her imbecile look.

On Sunday, went to Elliot's Beach for swimming, and extremely pleasant it was, and we went out on a catamaran and tried to shoot the surf coming back. But not very successful, as the man would not keep the catamaran straight. No sunset that day. The monsoon has now broken and there is plenty of rain.

The trouble here is bullock carts. They travel down the road at night in front of the bungalow, and their greaseless axles make a hideous noise, which wakes me up in the early morning. Then these Madrasis will shout when talking to a friend just six feet away.

Went out after snipe with Niven yesterday afternoon, on the Poonamallee road. I missed a couple, he missed a few and killed one. There were quite a few about though, and it rained during the shoot, and I felt that I might be in Aberdeenshire.

November 5th 1939

SOME MORE SHOOTING IN THE SAME SPOT – Ray and I and Nizam. Nizam killed and halaled a couple, rather like a good retriever. I fail to break my duck of course. I go down yachting with the Colonel. "Thistle" is Tomtit class, 18ft long, Bermuda rig and centreboard. I am instructed in putting about and in jibing, round and about the harbour. The famous 'Pansy' is there, looking rather like the minesweeper she was during the last war. Beer follows, and I apply to join the Club. Met one Dunn, of Wilts.

Went down yesterday and was more successful, though there was a bit of a wind blowing. In returning to our moorings, the Colonel brought her up, the paid hand pulling on the topping lift, and then I think I still had the main sheet, and he nearly went overboard. She listed right over, and the Colonel and I were just about to scramble onto the keel when she came up again. Went to an RAF hanger dance last night – not much good, as I didn't know anyone, so I left at 11.30 and returned to bed.

November 10th 1939

MADRAS

AN AWFUL RAINY DAY YESTERDAY. John and I went to the flicks at 6.00 pm and the Connemara afterwards, where I was introduced to a "Highball". A woman came in with another couple, whom we know as the 'S' bend, as that's how she looks when she's dancing. She observed our observation of her and eventually sent over Bannerji to ask if either of us would dance – John had one, I attempted one, in spite of the old man 'thumbing' me away. Eventually John goes over for another dance and the old man does some more 'thumbing' and tells him to go back to his kennel. After a bit of an argument the old man apologises, and asks John to go to dinner – I join them and get invited too. His name is Tingle of the Asbestos Cement company, and his wife thinks she is a bit of a vamp. She's a bit of a load to dance with, as she clings from the belly downwards, which I always find impedes forward movement.

November 13th 1939

MADRAS

I SEE IN THE "STATESMAN" THAT RAZCOL were in the Shaktu in October, and had two killed and eleven wounded – also an R.P. picquet was shot up on November 2nd and one killed with four wounded.

Yesterday went shooting with Ray, and got six snipe – he got seven. During one drive they were coming straight at me but I couldn't shoot them, as all the beaters were looking down the other end of my gun. I pretended to be a blade of grass and shot them overhead. Result was horrid, I only got one. I let off about twelve rounds rapidly, and couldn't load fast enough. Came back and the band was playing in the mess. I had invited the Spocket out (Celia Mockett), being the only girl I know in Madras, but I met one Mrs Hughes, an Australian.

Some days ago I went up to the Aerodrome and signed on for some flying. Tyndall-Briscoe, the instructor, gave me some ground instruction, and yesterday up I went for twenty mins dual, the first time in my life in the air, bar 5/- worth at Yeadon aerodrome some years ago. Went up to about 1000 feet and I took her over for a bit, and got a bit lost up there. Diving, climbing and steep turns seem rather to detach the pit of my stomach and I take it off too early, though I hope to god I will get out of that soon. I feel just like a chota peg[1] when I come down, but I managed with a cigarette instead.

I can't do any more dual until the medical form is filled in, and the damn man Hubbard won't do it until tomorrow. They also want a little bit in advance, the sharks.

I see that Gilbert R.A. got an MC for services in 1936-37, and Payne 2/7 and Doc Murray were mentioned for good work. Wrote to Mickey Wardle to see if there's a medal yet, but don't expect an answer. No vacancy for me at Sangar, and the Retention exam is suspended for the duration, so I have no 'homework' to do.

[1] *Miniature jug used for individual servings of alcohol, Chota is the Hindi word for 'small measure'.*

November 21st 1939
MADRAS

WENT UP FOR TWO TWENTY-MINUTE SHIFTS on Sunday – climbing and gliding turns, and then T.B. went up to 2000 feet and shook me about. I could take a climb and roll alright, but a spin rather caught me in the eardrums. Today did a bit of landing and taking off. There was a sufficient wind blowing to stall her at half throttle. There's plenty of water about on the ground, so if I ever get her up solo I'm going out to look at the sea.

Three BORs (British other ranks) killed and eleven wounded withdrawing from a picquet at Razmak on R.P., so says the Statesman.

This flying costs 30/- an hour dual, and I have now got in 1.5 hours – I feel happy in the air, only I can't land and take off yet, being unable to estimate height and gliding distance. A letter from Bill the other day. He is back in Palestine, and got his truck blown up by a mine not so long ago.

November 24th 1939
MADRAS

DINED WITH THE WILTS IN THE FORT the other night. Did us very well on pate de foie gras, asparagus and champagne. Played darts afterwards and I defeated Jack Newton, their QM and champ. Colonel Freeland observed doing a very smart hornpipe with himself. Last night dined out with Jimmy Smythe and Mrs, who is going to U.P. (Uttar Pradesh) as Military Secretary.

More hornpiping by the Col. ably supported by the others, and Rangru was made to conduct the band. I let off a brace of marriage bombs, which didn't go down too well.

Went up for half an hour on Thursday morning. Started off doing landings and take offs, but I mucked up my turns on the preliminary circuit, and spent the morning doing turns instead. Tyndall-Biscoe is a yogi I believe, and dines on orange juice and spring onions or some such combination. As long as he doesn't go into the 7th transportation at 2000 feet.

I look after the feeding and it's some job keeping my bearer up to the mark. He sabotaged last night's dinner, by making oyster patties out of oyster paste. Am getting a bit bored with this job. How I shall ever last twenty years of it I shudder to think. And what the hell will I be like at the end of it – heaven forbid that I ever become a 'typical army officer', especially an Indian army one. Waziristan was alright – and it didn't much matter where your puttees ended – but here, Christ! The Navy's the place for me – I always was interested in ships and it's a skilled job, whereas what I do now – its useful value is approximately nothing!

We go off to camp on Wednesday, so that might shake my ideas up a bit. We never got that dinner out of Tingle, the Cement King, as he rang up and said the Vamp was ill with fever – like hell. Jerry and I went and called on Westmoreland-Woods the other day – one daughter by the name of Elizabeth. With great difficulty obtained a whisky and soda and left.

December 1st 1939

Uttapanayskanna

In camp at Uttapanayskanna. Had a very pleasant fifteen mins flight before leaving the Mount. Did everything correct, including take-off and landing, and next time will be landing circuits, if T.B. remembers. Went out with Maitland to Barrington-Smith for a drink, and stayed to dinner. He and Maitland are a pair, and I reckon I am on sufferance only because of Harrow – they talk of English country houses and of English families and listen to me eagerly when I say what I know of the McLean hereditary litigation – but a damn fine dinner all the same, and it's the first time I have dined in someone's house in India, I think.

We leave the Mount on Wednesday 29th at 2.30 pm in two trains. I go in first with Golly, Niven and Beale. We dine at Villipuram, which is dinner for three provided by Spencer's man, and eaten by four hungry bodies. I meet Spencer's man there and have a talk with him. Arrive at Uttapanayskanna at 7am, and I get the bearer to work on breakfast, which he does fairly successfully. The second train arrives with Reggie Steward and D Coy, whose Indian officers come up and introduce themselves to me.

I then try to pack the Mess on the bullock cart transport which is waiting – QM has allotted one cart for the Mess and BOs baggage – but after much swearing and berating of drivers I eventually get it all off on seven carts. Am a bit worn out as it's very hot and then we have to march up here – about seven miles from the station. The road is a cart track, full of red dust, and I walk behind a mule. I find it impossible to keep time with the pipes and drums and their rifle regiment step, and march in step with the mule instead – long, slow and easy. The worst march I ever did, and the hardest worked day since I left Waziristan. The colour of Sahdu Singh's beard when we arrive is a good sight.

I have a 80lb tent – on hire – and have pinched a mess table. Also have boxes a la Razani, so am fairly comfortable. Hills all around here, so it looks like mountain warfare, and the place is being turned into a semi-perimeter camp. We have got (the CO arranged it) a mess car at four annas a mile, and twelve annas a day for the local driver, or give him bata. Also a frigidaire from detachment in Trichinopoly, which works by paraffin and will be a godsend in this heat. The war still goes on I believe.

December 5th 1939

Uttapanayskanna

"C" COMPANY DID A BIT OF MOUNTAIN WARFARE yesterday. I was horrified at it, but perhaps the methods I was taught are wrong after all. Anyway, no one will believe a word I say about it. Did a bit of field firing and ordered the local police to clear the range area by, say, 6.00 am. We then have to clear it ourselves, and start shooting around 7.30, having been just about to start once before and observed a man in dhoti up above one of the targets.

Two fat black policemen arrive at 9.30 and say sorry, had made mistake but now alright. One platoon has just finished firing and a local is then seen crossing the area, nearing the targets. I grab the arm of the fattest man and point a quivering finger at the apparition and threaten to get him sacked. He says 'excuse please' a few times and then sends his friend off to clear him out. The local is then seen doubling back out of the area like a frightened hare. We then ask fatty if we may start firing again. He says 'yes' so we ask him if he wants his friend to be killed – he had forgotten him, who is this moment coming back down the middle of the range.

Went into Madurai on Sunday to watch hockey against the police. Went in the back of a police lorry and nearly shaken to death. There had tea with Hamilton D.S.P. *(Deputy Superintendent of Police)* and drinks after the game. Whenever the D.S.P. happens to stand and talk to someone his Sergeant Major, a madrasi, falls in two men behind him. Hamilton looks around, they look a bit sheepish, so he asks the SM what the hell they are doing. SM answers 'to keep the sun off you, sar!'

Came back in the mess car which we have hired for four annas a mile and the driver's food, which is exceptionally good I think. After a hairraising drive in which we take the hair off a few old men and the driver strains her, by refusing to change down, we reach home, having got stuck in the sand whilst taking Golly back to his camp, where A and B Coys are. A letter from Ma, enclosing one she had from Peggy, who is by way of being the girl that Hugh married – Peggy, Pegs – I wonder!

December 11th 1939
UTTAPANAYSKANNA

WENT AND CLIMBED ONE OF THE LOCAL HILLS yesterday with Palmer and Awal Khan. We worked up a chimney but got foxed near the top and had to come down, making great use of Awal Khan's pagri *(turban)* as a rope. We then play football in the afternoon against the Madurai police in Usilampatti. They play in bare feet, and their goalkeeper gets his big toe badly cut by a boot. In fact the ball becomes bloody. After the game we wait from 5.30 to 7.30 in the police station for the home bus to arrive and pick us up – never again!

After having been instructed in bridge by Golly in St Thomas's Mount, I now find myself playing every night and am 58 annas up – Kent, the Doctor is 60 up and everyone else is minus.

Am getting a bit worn out here. Rise at 6.30 on parade from 7 to about 10, and get breakfast at 10.30, a barbarous hour – out again at 3.00 pm for about two hours, and then generally playing bridge up to about 11.00 pm – I can't take it.

There is very little scrub here, it is all cactus, of the bleeding sort, which drips milk and has an all round defence, so that you can't grasp it without being pricked. An answer to my letter to Bill

Webber, saying come when you like, but not especially enthusiastic. I think.

December 16th 1939

WENT INTO MADURAI AND PLAYED FOOTBALL there, where we defeated the local champions 5-4. After that, the secretary and D.S.P., one whose name in Tamil means 'God Help Us', took John and I to the station waiting room and got us pretty tight before dispatching us back in the lorry with the team. That morning I had gone out at 2.30 am on a night scheme, but got back in bed by 8.00 am until 12 midday, and didn't manage to football too badly after that.

The battalion did a twenty one mile march the other day – I wear boots for the first time in camp and collect a fine crop of blisters. We do a flag march to Madurai on 21st, so God help me if my feet aren't OK as it's all of thirty miles, and parade through the town afterwards. Willie Armstrong arrived today from Staff College. The Illustrated papers are out from home, and God how it pulls to read about this war. Off to Madurai today.

December 20th 1939

WENT INTO MADURA WITH THE COLONEL and Golly – I was due to stay with one Doakes, manager of the mill and drawing 6000/- a month. I arrive at his house, a palace set on the highest hill around Madurai, and with a wonderful view, if it wasn't an Indian one, and find no one there, he being still at his office. I have the sort of 7th guest bedroom, but it has all modern conveniences and a pair of good Persian carpets. I have tea, look longingly at the swimming pool, and then drink the breeze from the highest point for a considerable time.

Eventually Doakes arrives, but doesn't expect me, as I should be with some others in the mills, the Essex's, who have arranged a party for me. I shift house and meet them at the Khatak dance we put on – then back to dinner at the Essex's. They have a Swiss girl – Hildegard – up from Tuticorin for my partner. During dinner Mrs Essex gets pretty tight, she is an Australian with a cockney accent. And we go on to the club dance at about 10.00 pm, everyone pretty tight, bar me and the Swiss miss, and calling me "Lootenant". Return from dance at 3.00 am having done pretty well keeping Swiss miss out of hands of proletariat – John and Reggie & co. We five are the only ones from the Regiment – and do pretty well in the Palais Glide, where Golly and John bend back so far they crash to the floor amidst loud applause.

Arrange to shoot with Doakes in the morning, but on waking up I can't take it, and don't go. Leave Essex's at 2.00 pm and home with the Colonel and Golly in the car. Out that night at 1.00 am until about 9 – sleep 10.30 am until about 4.00 pm and out again at 1.00 am, in bed midday until about 5.00 pm. Then last night in bed. I didn't mind going out at night in Razmak – there were bullets about, you knew that, and it made it more interesting. But climbing through cactus after 'Popeyekanoor' or 'Sodapaniswami' – I would rather stay in bed.

Last night Madurai came here to a drinks party, but some shite in the S.P.M.R., and the Mills I suppose, brought out the Swiss miss and kept her all the time. A pretty good party, and Mrs Essex in great form. They all reckon to come and laugh at us when we march into Madurai, thirty miles, on 22nd. General Norton arrived today to watch the company field firing scheme. He chooses C Coy, and as Pearson is manager, I have to do it. God knows what will happen – or I don't – and a night scheme tonight to catch one "Champagne". I shouldn't feel much like marching after that, to Madurai.

December 25th 1939

THE NIGHT OPP. GOES OFF FAIRLY SUCCESSFULLY, and we start for Madurai at 4.00 am – arriving at 4.00 pm – 31.5 miles in all and with a stop for one hour. I find it pretty bloody on the feet, everything else being alright, but the Dogras look after me and feed me with fruit all the way. In Madurai we camp on the police football ground, and John and I nip off to the Essex's for a bath. I have two beers and one whisky there – then whisky in the club – and when I get to Brisley's the Collector's where we all dine, I feel bloody, but just manage to last the course, by consuming lots of lime juice during dinner. Next morning we march through Madurai, saluting the Collector on the way. All the locals (Essex's et al) are grouped solemnly on the saluting base, but I manage to keep a straight face, and pass grimly out of their lives (maybe).

Received Christmas card from Guy Hamlet, now on the staff in Quetta, also one from Biddy. Leicesters are in Agra now I hear. Arrived back here yesterday morning and went straight up to the aerodrome, where I did landing circuits, fairly successfully, though I was inclined to misjudge my glide, and had to use a bit of engine, or found myself overshooting. Had twenty minutes in the afternoon too, and find I am lighter on the stick, but a bit heavy with my feet.

December 28th 1939

A PARTY OF FOURTEEN FOR CHRISTMAS in the Connemara (25th) – British officers and two wives (Abbots and Rays) – pretty awful party, although Freeland got a bit foxed. However, later on some drunks from the B.I. line ships officers (British India Steam Navigation Company), arrived and seemed to collect around Abbott. One said to him "Where do I get a good ...". He pointed to his wife Rosemary and said "Over there". The chappie lurched over to Rosemary and said "Are ye on?". They all had fearful Glasgow accents, and Abbott's wife was furious, though he thought it rather funny. Willie and I, John and Pat Irwin went on to the Gymkhana Club afterwards.

Willie and I shouldn't have gone, as John wanted to get on and do some necking. Then two lads off the "Silver U" arrived, a 3rd mate and an electrician. They were 72 days out from New York across the Atlantic and Indian Ocean, and hadn't seen a woman all that time. I took the wind out of their sails by telling them of ten months in Waziristan and never saw one.

Got to bed at 5.00 am, and flying cleared my head at 9.30. Went sailing with Willie and Abbott, doing flying and sailing the same day, which I wanted to do. Yesterday John and I were invited to an early night do in the Connemara by May Green, one of the Horrors. Her husband, John's hairdresser friend, and Lt Hart (Royal Indian Navy) were present. Later (less husband) we went to the Gym Club, where I nearly got tight, having drunk whisky in the Connemara, as they started on champagne and then brandies came round. Had a very good 1.5 hours flying this morning, only it's a little bumpy.

December 31st 1939

MADRAS

FLYING AND SAILING, AND THE OTHER DAY Willie landed me on the 'Kallerati' ('Calamity' – her sister ship 'Deepuali' being the 'Depravity'). Had tea with one Sweet-Escott (Subaltern R.I.N.V.R.) He showed me over the works, and then Hart and the hairdresser Rene arrived, just as I went ashore.

Last night John and I went to the cinema and on from there to the Connemara. There John encountered Mr and Mrs Gordon (railways) and we spent the evening and night with them. Left Connemara at midnight and went to the Gymnkhana Club, where

93

a fancy dress dance was in progress, with lots of drunks. Bed by 3.30 am – a few drinks in the Gymkhana, and then I did some useful elbow work and seized the Connemara cabaret star, much to the disgust and envy of those around and about. Forgot to ask her if she was married!

Gordon has done 150 hours solo, and took seventeen hours dual before it, so it doesn't look like I shall have much chance of going solo for many a month yet. Letters from Bill, Hugh and Peggy, and three handkerchiefs from Mrs Robinson. *(CDW's friend Bill's mother).*

January 3rd 1940

MADRAS

WENT TO DINNER WITH MAJOR MONEY – and then on to the Connemara and Adyar Club for the New Year. Connemara packed with a lot of lads, who looked as if they had only been there once, and that was last New Year's Eve. Saw the New Year in at the Adyar – it's like an old country house and is most beautifully decorated, the only drawback being the Governor's band, who perform none too well. Met Celia Mockett there and fixed up a flick for Tuesday – I collected her at Tippoo, and we saw 'Snow White'. After that, returned to Connemara and found I had made a balls up and it was Jack Bontemps' off day.

However, Celia suggested the Madras Club, so off we went there for drinks on her! On reckoning things out, it's the very first time I ever took a girl out, excluding Daphne of course, as she generally took me in her car. Funny that!

Am going off to camp for three weeks with the Wilts, as an umpire, though all the umpiring I ever did was that course of Jimmy's, and one day (or rather night) at Uttapamayakkannor. The weather nice and cool now, and there's a paper in from Waz District that we move on February 28th or so, arriving Wana via Manzai on 7th March. Saw in the intelligence summary that

Wanacol got heavily sniped one day recently, while out on column – that looks hopeful, but Golly doesn't seem to think much of the Wana Wazirs, at least not as fighting men.

What a difference in one's life good friends make. Here am I, having spent 21 years living behind a sort of mask of suspicion and social fright, and here I am sort of received with open arms and it's all gone. The Leicesters didn't do that, and with them I used to get pangs of annoyance, mistrust and even hatred sometimes, which I hadn't felt since dark days at Harrow. Certainly not at the R.M.C. *(Royal Military College, Sandhurst)*. All that is now gone, for ever I hope. I have even found my tongue – at times!

She is a nice girl, that Celia is.

January 7th 1940

In camp near Puttur

IN CAMP WITH THE WILTS, AS AN UMPIRE, near Puttur – until 27th, dammit. Went solo on 4th at 6.30 am – T-B took me for a couple or so (three) chukkers first – dual – and then I did a couple solo, ten minutes in all. Beyond a great inclination to sing, which I did, there was no difference in it at all. Have now done five hours ten minutes dual, which is reckoned as pretty good, the normal pre-solo dual being about eight hours.

Came down here on Friday, and the only good thing about it that I can see is that in the Mess they have the London Times, which I haven't seen since before the war. The camp is situated under trees, on which all sorts of birds sit and make a bloody noise at night. One end is bounded by the road, and the other by paddy fields. It would be alright for mountain warfare, provided each man left his rifle behind and took a machete instead, as the hills are covered in thorn scrub, much thicker than any of that cactus at Uttapanayakkannor. The B.O.s seem to do pretty well, one even brought a chest of drawers along, but they don't seem to take much trouble over washing as they have no bath tent and we use these

95

bloody camp baths. However, I manage to borrow a tin bath from Lees-Smith, who brought his own.

I have a 160lb tent, and God knows what it will cost. At present Hamilton ('Dopey') is giving his bearer hell for not understanding that "1. pencil, 2. foolscap" written on a piece of paper does not mean one pencil and two sheets of paper. I reckon I shall hit him before long if I'm not careful, and fail to control my temper.

January 12th 1940

In camp near Puttur

STILL IN THIS BLOODY CAMP and about another fortnight to do. I have been safety officer on some field firing exercise, alongside a bit of umpiring, but I might just as well be in Madras for all the work I'm doing here. On Friday went out twelve miles, spent the night, and marched back yesterday – at least the Wilts did, but I went out in a lorry and back in the Doctor's (Keyes) car. Spent the night with Jos Redman, who was the 'enemy', near Nagari, I being the enemy's umpire. Had dinner at Battalion HQ and drove out to where the enemy were spending the night, round a good fire. He lent me a blanket, as I only had my cardigan, and it was about eight or nine feet long, so I was able to wrap up pretty well in it.

We drink whisky for a couple of hours before turning in, and we discuss marriage, he being engaged and due for splicing in a few months. A bloody cold night, and up at 4.30. Very few chaps slept, owing to the cold that night, but I did fairly well, and on the Battalion getting back at about 2 pm a lot of the young officers departed to bed, had supper there, and appeared again the next morning for breakfast. Attam Khan *(Colin's bearer)* asks what's wrong with them, having only spent the one night out, and what would happen if there was a war on (?!) and they didn't get any rations for a couple of days.

A lot of holy monkeys round here, who live in the trees, and are known to climb up the tent ropes and then slide down the canvas sides. Also flying foxes. At last got licenses for my shotgun and a .22 Colt, with five hundred free cartridges, though I hate to think what the price of them will be just now at P. Orr's. No hope of getting back to Madras early, as some of the regiment are coming here on the 26th as enemy, but I am the only one here who can speak the language. Captain Crocker, Inniskillins, known as 'Hobo', is the other umpire.

January 18th 1940

In camp near Puttur

ANOTHER NIGHT OUT WITH JOS as enemy umpire. Went out at 10.00 pm and back by 11.00 am. We sat near a village and then went up a hill amongst the cactus. Never slept a wink owing to the cold. Used up Jos's iron rations – whisky! A letter from Ray, telling me to behave myself in this camp and explaining things. I sent a letter to Abbo. *(Battalion HQ in Abbottabad)* saying I didn't consider I was really wanted here, and would be more use at the Mount. However, I think I've been a bit of a B.F. One good thing – I think I mentioned before – is that they have the 'Times' in the Mess here. A letter from Aunt Vivy enclosing 10/- shillings for Christmas – a cheque.

January 31st 1940

Madras

RETURNED BACK ON THE 28TH. The intelligence section of the 2nd Frontier Force Rifles came down on the 26th for a scheme on the night of the 27th. This was the General's test scheme of the Wilts. I umpired Mickey Thomas. Hobo, Adrian Cooke and Tim

Money also arrived. Next day the General finished his talk at 3 pm. I left at 3.05 and the General at 3.06. Met Cotterill on return, and then Downe arrived from Lahore to join – he reminds me of Hamilton somewhat.

Went flying on Sunday – not much good – also Monday and Tuesday before parade, but I have lost the feel and bog all my landings. I do one solo circuit and try to land about five feet above the ground – a hell of a bump.

Went into Madras today and bought five hundred .22 cartridges at 3/8 a hundred. Also three "life buoys" @ four annas each. So now hoping for big stuff to come. Am living in Wilts officers quarters as everything else is taken. Feeling bloody minded about this flying, as all a damn waste of time and money, when I could land so well before I went away. I think I leave it too long before 'flattening out'. Just got Biddy's photo – I don't like it at all.

February 4th 1940

MADRAS

WENT TO ADYAR TEA DANCE given by the Sprocketts. John and I went with Appleton in his car. A couple of new RAF boys, "Dickie" Bird and "Peggy" O'Neill, arrived. The Wilts band performed, and the drummer boy had a high seat and grinned at all the women. One girl I danced with, Eve Maynard, I had to manoeuvre so she could see him. Not being a member of the joint, with difficulty I obtained two chota pegs, and when it finished at 8.30 pm we went to the Connemara – the two RAF chaps, myself, Celia, Daphne, Eve and one Joan Swann. John had found some'at else. When all finished, we went on to the Gymkhana, returning to bed about 01.30.

Thursday played squash with Jim Robbins. A training aircraft crashed the other day whilst the pilot, an Indian, was 100 feet off the ground, at some provincial landing ground. He got windy of the enquiry and on his statement put that he could remember nothing until he woke up in hospital. The machine was written off. Did a couple of chukkers solo yesterday and getting better, I hope. Whilst getting into one of those Blenheims the other day, one of the pilots accidentally pressed a button and the guns started off, pointing towards Madras!

On Friday 2nd we give our farewell "cocktail dance". Flowers arrive and I spend the morning helping Mrs Springfield and Jane with them. The racecourse lend us 'Pots, plants containing' and their head gardener fits them up in a few minutes. We hire a shamiana *(Urdu: an outdoor marquee for entertaining)* for the bar, the Wilts band in the ballroom and ours in the garden. John's room is, suitably, used as the Ladies room, and they all admire his photo round the walls.

Before the guests arrive, Lt Beale observed the shamiana boy concocting a 'white lady', brooding about alchemists and their work and wondering why it turned pink? They all arrive, about 150 of them. We are drawn up on the verandah at 8 pm, B.O.s and wives. His Excellency de-busses to 'God Save the King', and then shakes hands all down the line. After that – let the play commence. I have a dance or two with Celia, Daphne and then catch Marjorie Buller. Having hidden a few Pink Ladies (Colin's strategy to avoid peaking too early was to 'park' drinks) I am in crashing form, beating old boys on the back and telling them they look thirsty and explaining to dames that we don't keep no soft drinks here. Marjorie in cracking form too and I walk her "out of the out gate and into the in" – but nothing doing.

There's a supper bar in the eating room, and in the Frippets room a first class dining saloon for the Governor and those selected as fit by his ADCs. Sidelights – William had a gap in his conscious mind from 11.30 pm until he woke up in the morning. I got to bed at one and then up again to go flying at 6am. Yesterday took Sprockett to the cinema and the Connemara afterwards, but as I was suffering from Boozers Gloom, not very satisfactory.

February 6th 1940

Madras

HAD A DAMN GOOD FLIGHT TODAY, before parade, at 6.30 hrs – did two chukkers dual, as T-B didn't like my first landing, which I nibbled at, as I saw a plane going the other day in the dusk. Then did four chukkers, perfect, though maybe two landings were a bit pancaky.

We all went to a cocktail party given by Maj-Gen Wilson ICS, yesterday in Guindy – encountered Michael Hunter, going to France on Sunday, and Mickey Thomas, met Pam Holdsworth, looked at, in the way that dogs do (as not officially introduced) Anne Maconachie, and Jean Gordon. Maitland's friend, Marjorie Buller, arrived too, whom I looked after last Friday. Well, I sit and talk to her the whole time, and produce excerpts from my experiences in Waziristan. Come back slightly whistled and have a drink off Cotterill after dinner, in company with Bill. Being slightly afloat, as I say, I sit down after dinner and write Marjorie a letter, she having said how she adores them. I start "Dear Sir – " and explain I was writing to the bank but somehow I seem to be writing to her – hadn't I better see a doctor about it? In the light of day, I go to the post box to get it back, and find to my horror it has gone. No harmful effects, I hope. Later she rings me up – delighted with it.

February 8th 1940

Madras

YESTERDAY I WAS ALLOWED TO TAKE OFF from the beginning, solo. They put out the sheet and round I go. I don't like the look of the first one, so round I go again. Just as I am turning in, I see the leopard about to take off, so I do a small circle right. I am still gliding, am not paying attention, and she begins to stall at 100-200 feet! I give her her nose and some engine, then full engine, round and land. Coope nearly had a fit as high tension wires were underneath!

This morning T-B has one chukker dual, then OK, and off I go – I now have 1.10hrs solo. This morning Dr Dyson took me off for thirty five minutes as observer whilst we attacked the minesweepers. We went out to sea, they were a mile or two off land, and came down from the sun and a cloud at 3500 feet. He did glides and stall turns, then we circled for a torpedo attack and back home – delightful. I spot Freeland on one with my field glasses.

Last night a dance at Government House. John, Jerry, Tony Cotterill, Downe and myself all go in Tippoo (dressed up), and arrive to be the only ones in a soft shirt (I originally had silk shirt and cummerbund, but had to change them again). Had a good time, a few cocktails, supper with Celia and some dancing with Marjorie Buller. I also walk her out twice around dark and dim bushes, but she won't kiss me – though I give her a peck for luck. I am reputed to be mad here, so these frippets think, but I explain how I have only three more weeks in civilisation. Sent Marjorie a cap badge, with my love of course.

February 12th 1940

MADRAS

THURSDAY NIGHT PADRE JOHN and I went to the Connemara after dinner for a quick one. Met old Ruffle, who invited us to his party – pretty bloody awful, as I didn't feel like drinking and was rather tired. So Ruffle, who was in a worse condition, and I, drank Rose's lime juice. Hart, R.I.N. (Royal Indian Navy), and three hairdressers there. I dance with one Renee, so small you can hardly see her. Friday we all go to the garden party at Government House. The Governor arrives down a lane of bodyguards with the "old guard", including the C.O., drawn up to receive him – sing God Save the King – and we get down to it. The tea is foul so I drink orange juice. All the Indian stuffing themselves with both hands as

101

hard as they could go. We all walk round and chat about this and that, I and Marjorie and the rest. Then I go back with Padre and Downe, the rest of the boys going to the Connemara, for an early night with Major and Mrs Springfield. I drink beer with them and then to bed.

Saturday sailing with Willie in "Thistle". We have a hell of a race with Low and Gibbs in Lapwing. But local knowledge and the better sailing of Low wins the day, though we lead on the start and nearly catch him up again on the second time round from Cassinode to Seamark. "Thistle"'s mast isn't stepped right and Lapwing just sails faster than we do on the port tack. We keep the spinnaker up as extra jib during the last home stretch, but his lead is too great and he gets away.

Back at 6.45 pm and off to a cocktail party in the Fort, given by Steve and Mickey Thomas to some of their lads who are going off to France, including Michael Hunter. I sit and talk to Marjorie for a bit and then she goes home, I having fixed a date at the "Gym" with her for 10.30 pm. I have had three gin and limes with water and feel damn drunk. I then have dinner in the Wilts Mess (free I hope) and then go along to the Sergeants Mess where I meet Sgt Webber, an old friend from Camp. RSM Milsom not there disafortunamente. Have a lime pani *(lime juice)* and feel sober again. Major Lloyd RIASC passes out on the floor and then I go to the Gym in Gibb's car, my own Royal Taxi having disappeared. Here I meet John and the Hughes' in whose party Marjorie is. I refuse all offers to booze, manage to collect Marjorie for a couple of dances and then push off.

I manage to get Mr Spencer's, presumably THE Spencer's, driver to drive me home, give him 5/- and am in bed by 1.00 am.

Saturday morning I go flying twenty minutes solo. T-B shows me the figures of eight. I try at 600 feetand in fifteen minutes have reached 1200 feet. I glide down and try again. When landing I am a bit tired and heavy, and only just pull up in time as she hits the ground. She bounces, I put on some engine, and eventually she flops to a rest. I notice a twitch in my left knee as I climb out – why?

At 10.15 Marjorie picks me up in the car of one Leslie Cooper, and off we go for a picnic at The Seven Pagodas (Mahabalipuram), some 45 miles from here. We stop and repair the back brake on the way, but eventually arrive at the canal, which is crossed in a sort of houseboat after much garbar *(Urdu: negotiation),* the cars being left this side – Mr and Mrs Buller, Annette and husband, Steve and Jean Gordon, Eve Maynard and Leslie Cooper. We bathe and have a picnic lunch in the Collector's bungalow. Then we look at the Five Rathas, have tea and it's time to come home. Casuarinas, acacias and some other flowers make the whole place particularly beautiful. There's a nice place for bathing, with rocks reminiscent of Tiree. I see a pleasant picture of a small cove with a long beach one side, and in the foreground this side a huge rock just at the water's edge, with palm trees at the edge of the beach, and Marjorie and Eve washing the sand off their feet in the sea. They wave to me to come down, and I wonder when I shall see such a scene, and in such a setting, again. Shades of Tiree, but there I had no picture for my frame!

A very nice drive back with Marjorie in the back seat. She gives me a hand and we talk sweet nothings. Forty five miles, a fine sunset, a bit of a moon, but it has to end at St Thomas's Mount.

February 13th 1940

Madras

YESTERDAY WILLIE AND I WENT OUT to train for the Ladies Race in the regatta next Monday. I asked Pat Turner, she said she was away, but try Ann Maconachie. Ann said she was already booked, but try Bang-my-arse, who said she would be seasick, but try Elsie Wadsworth. I have never met her, but ring her up and explain all this. We eventually take her out, and she's not too bad,

Willie managing the mainsheet and I manipulating the jib and mast halyards. We have a drink at her house in Nungambankam on the way home, and meet Ma and Pa – also some beautiful Persian carpets. Letter from Pop Jacobs yesterday, enclosing £2.

February 16th 1940

Madras

WENT TO A COCKTAIL PARTY in the Connemara, given by Jimmy Jamieson, the other day. I invited myself on Celia's suggestion. Not a great success. Stayed on with Marjorie afterwards then took her home, and she gave me one of Pa's whiskies. Almost engaged to T.R. Molloy of Northampton in Jhansi, whose badge she wears.

Yesterday went out flying in the morning, doing figure of eight's over the ranges fairly successfully, even though I pulled the stick in a lot to swing her round, and might have stalled and spun when coming out of the turn. Entered Elsie for Ladies Race, so Willie and I took her down in the afternoon. Fifteen knot breeze, but we had a bad start and finished last of the Tomtits (a class of sailing boat). Saw a huge turtle in the harbour. Rushed back to Bearen's cocktail party. They had a most villainous cocktail – I tried half but it seemed to be pure alcohol. Later on, John invited me to come with Celia and Joan Swann to Connemara – I said yes, and immediately invited Marjorie too. This made things uneven so I collected Gerald Dunn and off we went in Celia's car. We had a spot of dinner. I danced with Marjorie more than with the other two put together, but it really was fun.

Adrian Cooke, 'Franco' because of his sideboards, was throwing a party to celebrate his departure for France. Very drunk and yelling 'Viva!'. I replied with 'Zieg Heil!' and eventually he embraced me on both cheeks in correct continental style. Elsie asked me to a 'Lido' party tonight at Adyar – dressing as one would there (where? Brighton?). OK, I say, then Springheel says there's night firing tonight. I then have to tell Elsie I cannot make it before

9.15, but when I ask Springheel he kindly says I can go. I hope it will be alright.

Went dive-bombing today with Appleton in a Blenheim. She dived at 260 mph but I wasn't awfully impressed, and why Jerry was nearly sick I don't know. About four bombs stuck in the rack, so he went out to sea to try and unload them. This the gunner did, by opening a hatch and knocking them off with his hand. I was hoping he wouldn't be able to do so and that I should be 'bailed out'.

February 17th 1940

Madras

Did thirty mins solo at 5.00 pm yesterday – did figure of eights at 600 feetfairly successfully I think, though whether I can land on the mark I don't know. I did a few landings, sort of settle down ones, as it was a bit bumpy. Shut off at 1200 feetand landed, and took a look at the Mess. It was the best flight I ever had. Then I went out to the range and had a puncture and had to walk back. It took forty minutes, but I made 8.30 OK.

Wore white shirt, trousers, rugger blazer and a scarf – most chaps in shirt and trousers. Dined with the Wadsworths, plus Elsie and the two Mocketts and of course Marjorie, along with Steve, Jimmy, another Willie and a chap I didn't know. Some good beer for dinner and I upset my coffee cup on the table like a bloody fool. I find myself seated next to Marjorie at dinner. I was told to send the driver away as soon as I arrive, and am next told to take Marjorie in Wadsworth's car – everyone going in pairs – so I reckon Celia Mockett must have fixed that.

Arrive at Adyar and find it's a programme dance. Get mine (his dance card) filled with a few horrors, but allow three for Marjorie. Sign S. Marmaduke on a drink or two, with his kind permission. There were chaps playing roulette, and there were lilos and mattresses everywhere. I take Marjorie for a walk or two and some more of her lipstick, though she isn't very helpful. I don't know why – I'm sure she likes it. Meet Willie Thyne (bart) who says I'm his rival. This goes on until 2.30 am when God Save the King is struck up. I'm pretty worn out, haven't seen Marjorie for a couple of dances, and pretty angry. Bill turns up, the Colonel having gone off for a weekend in Madurai with Doakes. He is with the Barrington-Smythes and Mrs Dyson. All five girls get in Wadsworth's car and take me home. No parades today thank god, so I get up at 8.30am.

February 20th 1940

MADRAS

FLYING AND SAILING – the flying not too good as I seem to misjudge my landings on the mark, even from 600 feet, as well as from 2000 feet. The eights aren't too bad, though they are not consistent at 600 feet. But today I try again, and land within 20 feet of the sheet every time but one, doing forty minutes altogether.

Yesterday took Elsie out in the regatta, both her and her sister and two Mocketts. Marjorie said she wanted to come too. We get beaten by Gibbs and Thyne. We have tea there, Willie, John and I (at 1/8 a head - christ!), and then Elsie drops me at the Maynards where I change before going on to the Connemara early night. The party consists of Mr and Mrs, another married couple, Leslie, Marjorie and Eve. Willie and John were there too, very drunk. Most enjoyable, and after 10 pm back to their house for sandwiches and beer. Chicken sandwiches, tongue and sausage rolls, and beer in tall thin cut glass tankards. Simply wonderful. Eve is a kind girl and sensible. Then Leslie takes me home, my suitcase is put on the front seat next to him, Marjorie gets in the back, and there's room for me too. A pleasant drive home, and I feel compelled to kiss her a few times properly. She seems more responsive than usual too. Back in bed by 11.45, after a damn good night.

Two new chaps in the Wilts come out from home – one Scarlett (Colonel!) is 30, was a civil servant before the war, is now a 2nd Lt. John and he and his pal and Dickie Bird gave a party on Elliott's beach the other night. I swam, it was rather pleasant, and the Colonel insisted in going in in his glasses and then wondered why he lost them in the surf. But Mrs Buller would not allow Marjorie to go. "No", she said to me, "I have to draw the line somewhere, and I draw it at moonlight picnics, until she's 21!" The poor sweet being now just 19. At about 12.30 pm a figure was seen lurching across the sand, and it turned out to be Bill in his pyjamas and dressing gown. He had gone to bed, and ordered a taxi surreptitiously and come on down to Elliott's beach.

February 22nd 1940

MADRAS

COMPLETED TESTS FOR MY 'A' LICENSE TODAY. Monday I was bloody awful, Tuesday I had all the tests taped, so I booked Wednesday 7.30 am with four hours solo. I did the eights but mucked up my landing, being too far from the sheet. The next two glides down from 2000 feetwere perfect, and I nearly stopped on the sheet itself. That afternoon did two eights and landed on the circle, and passed that test. My barograph was OK, as I kept at about 500 feet, but she looked a bit drunken during my figures of eight. Then a spinning test with T-B in, and this morning I go up to make thirty minutes and complete my five hours. I climb to 5000 feetand do right and left spins down to about 2300 feet, then back up to 4000 feetand one long spin, pulling out of the dive exactly on 2000 feet. I keep my eyes on the altimeter all through the spin, and feel no effects at all. The aerodrome officer then questions me on Indian Aircraft Rules, which lay down what sort of lights a captive balloon, broken away, being towed by a glider, must display, when looping the loop.

This afternoon rang up Marjorie to come out and have tea, as I have to go into Madras for my 'A' License photos. She said the Ludfords and Jane were lunching with her, she was bringing them home, and so would take me out. She comes out and we go off to the Yacht Club. We take a walk around the Mole and watch the turtles and the minesweepers and then have tea on the lawn. "Thistle" appears on the water with Willie, John and the Grinder. She gives me a letter, not to be opened until she is gone. She had intended to post it, as she didn't expect to see me again before the station. I open it in the taxi after having put her home, about 6 pm, and it's rather touching. I try to ring up, but can't express myself well enough, so write her a letter. She goes to Marmagoa, but back on Wednesday, so must see her that night I hope.

Padre, Arsitarsi, John and I go to Connemara in the evening. Meet the complete drunk – Capt P.G. Hennessey 4/10 Baluchis. Nodding head, slobbering at the mouth, swaying, shaking and pukka blurred speech. I get the Padre onto him and we get him to bed eventually, talking French, German, Urdu and Pashto. A bit of a clever chap.

February 26th 1940

MADRAS

GO SAILING ON SATURDAY. I skipper "Thistle" with Cotterill as crew, and we come last. He is sick at one period, the effect of bad whisky at an RAF dance last night, so he tells me. At Rajpuram I put about too quickly, and have to jibe to avoid hitting the buoy. I nearly capsize her once or twice too, and when letting down the sail at the end it catches on one of the wire hallyards and makes a tear about four inches long.

Then dinner with Jos Redman in the Fort, and we go to the Connemara afterwards with Mike Kerro, Cotterill and Scarlett. I don't enjoy it, have three gin slices and we get away about 1am. Abbott has a cocktail party that night, to which I am not invited,

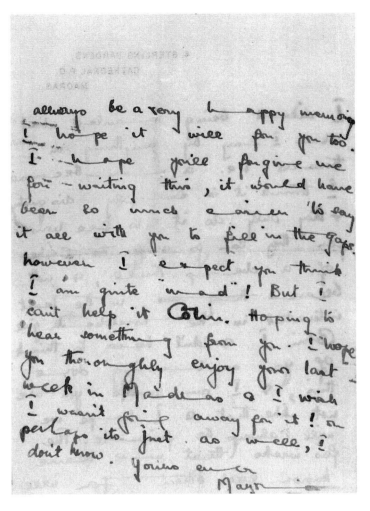

always be a very happy memory. I hope it will for you too. I hope you'll forgive me for writing this, it would have been so much easier to say it all with you to fill in the gaps. However I expect you think I am quite "mad"! But I can't help it Colin. Hoping to hear something from you. I hope you thoroughly enjoy your last week in Madras & I wish I wasn't going away for it! or perhaps it's just as well, I don't know. Yours ever Marjn

The last page of the letter from Marjorie, 'not be be opened until she is gone.'

and then they all arrive at the Connemara at about 11 pm. The only people I want to dance with are in that party, which makes it a bit awkward, and I can do nothing about it.

Last night John and I called on the Mocketts – having given warning – they don't seem very keen to see us...

February 28th 1940

MADRAS

WENT UP TO THE AERO CLUB the other afternoon and found Patterson Morgan and one Kathline Wilson having tea with T-B. I joined the party, and then he said go and show us what you can do. I went up to 4300 feetand spun to 2000 feet, then did stall turns very nicely. Most enjoyable it was too. Yesterday went to the station from 7.00 am – 3.00 pm, baggage loading, pretty bloody too. Breakfasted in the restaurant. Went to the Wilts Retreat and drinks afterwards. H.E. there. I had two whiskies and felt bloody. Bathed in Jos's room then Tony Cotterill and I went to dine with the Maynards and go on with the ADC's party to Government House afterwards. His Ex. there in the same suit he wore for the Retreat, less coat, as it was a 'Cool Kit' party. I became ill and was sick in the lavatory, then departed for bed. "Knees up Mother Brown" done by Douglas ADC, then we all tried our hands at it.

Marjorie back today so I arrange for her to come up to the Connemara early night and then on to the cinema, with a party of about eight. It's very nice to hear her voice on the telephone again, and I do hope it will be a good party, in spite of my illness. A bit of sleep will soon put that right though.

March 11th, 1940

WANA

JOHN, TONY, KING OF SWING AND I went to the Connemara on the last night. Two Mocketts, Wadsworths and Black Bess (as they call Marjorie), so we pick up Langford James there to make up numbers. We dance, eat fish and chips up top and then go to the

New Elphinstone (Madras's poshest cinema). Marjorie takes me in her car and I hold her hand in the cinema, being seated on two-seater sofas. Then to Gym (Club), where John is the only member and has to pay for all the drinks. I dance with Marjorie and back in bed by 1.30. Marjorie rather excitable and seems to be in rather a state, but prettier than ever.

On 29th I go down to the station at about 7.00 am and load baggage. Have breakfast, and lunch there at 3.00 pm. The farewells begin. Eve and Bang-me-Arse, and most of the Wilts. I catch old Buller eyeing me a bit queerly and have a word with him. Garlands of roses provided by Northland Sports Works, who provided us with kit in the Mount and took a lot of money off me. I am almost reduced to tears, and can only shake hands and chew my pipe. I then give Marjorie a quick kiss as the train moves off and get in quick. She gave me a horrid looking photo of her last night, suitably inscribed.

The journey is pretty bloody. I have Downe and Cotterill, and the latter goes ashore at Delhi, gets tight, and is sick on his bed last night – a horrid smell. I do a lot of thinking, and my life seems bloody. Why did I join the army? Any bloody fool could do this job, and there is no satisfaction of the craftsman in his trade. I could forget the journey quite happily.

Played football at Bhopal against State Forces on real grass, a polo field. First time since coming out here. Saw fourteen dead tigers in one lad's house. At Agra rushed off the train to see the Taj Mahal, but not looking very beautiful and fleeced of rupees at every turn. In Delhi we went to Cecil's Hotel with Major J.L. Jones, who made us drunk (John, Tony and I) and gave us a bath and dinner. The neighbourhood of AHQ and 'Marble Arch' reminded me of Harrogate Stray.

Arrived Mari Indus on the 6th, and I duly cross the bridge with Bill on foot. We are given tea by old pensioners in the Rest Camp. Spend two nights there, and reach Manzai on the 8th. A shocking place, where we spend two nights with the 3/8. Then a convoy to

Wana, and relieve 2/8 Gurkha Rifles. I pray for a hold-up – but nothing, though two shots were fired at 2/8 going down the day before in the Shahur Tangi (A defile where a British convoy was ambushed with heavy casualties in 1937 - see March 10th 1939). A grim place, the Shahur Tangi, and Mehr Dil (rebels) supposed to be about.

Met Lakri Woods, S.W.D. at Jandola. First glimpse of snow from Shahur Tangi above Spli Toi scout post. Wana is very bare, and full of heaps of broken bricks, dust and rubble. John about to be married in April, Jerry hoping to get a job at J.O.S. Sangur and marry Pat Turner, Bill off to the I.A.O.R. in two months or so, Willie and Abbott presumably off to Staff jobs, Paddy Keen expected to go back to Political, Reggie wanting S.W.S. A new 7/13 to be formed and B.O.s required for it. So it will be pretty bloody soon. When I got my "A" License I applied for seconding to the RAF and Freeland said he wouldn't hear of it ever, the old shite. I go on a gas course to Pachmari next month.

March 17th 1940

Wana

I HEAR THAT NO INDIAN ARMY BRITISH OFFICERS are allowed into the RAF. Michael Oliver here in 1/18, a Captain, also Pepe Savignon, Lyall, Arthur Murray, Collins, Taggart and Shaw. I am living in Gunners quarters. A bloody wind just now, like the old 'sting of death'. Reconstruction everywhere here, piles of muck and rubble and it all looks pretty bloody. The Brigade goes in ten days to camp in Karab Kot on 3rd April, which I shall miss unfortunately, as there may be some fun there. Have called on Gunners and Garhwalis (The Garhwal Rifles) and there are plenty more to do.

I buy a camera in the bazaar for 34/-, but haven't had much opportunity to use it so far. British officers commanding companies can be made acting Captain (to fill Battalion establishment) and if held for 21 days get paid too – but no one in this battalion has anything. The Army instruction is rather vague. It must depend on Freeland. Reading up on gas warfare. Jolly is a great help over this, with his A.R.P. booklets.

March 21st 1940

WANA

COTTERILL AND I HAD DINNER with the Gunners last night and then played poker with them. I got away with some money in my pocket. You never get outside this bloody perimeter except exercising – no R.P. There's shooting in Razmak, but not a thing here, although one Pir Nullah and his boys are reputed to be lying in wait for the Wana Hunt, wanting to kill a B.O.

Why did I join the army?

March 26th 1940

WANA

I GET SUDDEN ORDERS ONE NIGHT to go with the convoy leaving next morning, so have to pack in hell of a hurry. This gives me six days spare on the way, so I wire the Franklins in Jhansi that I am coming to stay with them. We get down to Mangai OK, then manage to catch the convoy to D.I.K. (Dera Ismail Khan) after lunch. Davidson, a dentist and I share a staff car. A deadly dull journey, a long straight road, a regular speed of 24 mph with the milestones and furlong posts slowly slipping by. A flat desert on each side, like the Mari Indus-Lakki Marwat stretch, only flatter, with hills in the distance. I shut my eyes and think of Tiree, and every detail of the house comes back, rather extraordinary, as I had never thought of it before.

Met Colonel Weld in the Club in DIK, had a drink with him and went to look up Jackson, Chief Clerk. He is out, so return to the Club. At about 11.00 pm Davidson and I set out in an old car for Darya Khan. We cross innumerable arms of the Indus, by boat bridges, and catch the midnight train to Lalamusa. He goes on to Lahore, I change for Delhi, change again and arrive at Jhansi 4.10 pm on the 24th.

The Franklins are staying in the Club, and I see them about 7.00 pm, only to discover they are heading for Bombay, and home the next day. I have dinner in the Club with Fenella (Fenella Franklin) and two of her admirers, Harry Lee of 2/18 and one Tony of the Northamptons. I spoil their tete-a-tete-a-tete and after dinner they leave eventually, one after the other. Fenella and I sit in the moonlight under a tree, and I play my cards wrong like the bloody fool I am. Anyway, both the other two sneak back to say goodbye properly, and I creep off to bed disgruntled.

I see the Franklins leave at 6.30 am, and that day I have never been so bored in years. Joe Nash is away, Gus Holland is in Bombay, and I have read all the papers in the Club. I wire Chemsie Motor Service and am leaving today for Pachmarhi, though I don't have to be there until 31st. How I feed I don't know, but it can't be a worse place than this. I see that Harry Browell is with the Warwicks in Razani, and that a platoon sergeant won a DCM at Lower Tambre Obo! – my first Razani picquet.

March 31st 1940

PACHMARHI

I ARRIVE HERE ON 27TH, AND AS THE MESS is not open I stay at the Pachmarhi hotel, very pleasant. It's fairly cool here, and a sight for sore eyes after Wana. Rolling 'downs', trees and a church spire topping it off make a picture like England. A sweet smell from the trees too. I play alot of tennis in the Club, next door, and swim in the Club pool. A couple called Shipway are in the hotel – IAOC, late 4/8 of Razmak, and knew it well. Strallan's commandant of this school, with a glamourous daughter called Joan – engaged to Henson of KOSB *(Kings Own Scottish Borderers)*. She's just adopted make-up on the strength of her engagement, and none too skillful in its application. Pam Shallow is also here, her Pa being Lt Col of AEC School. Went to call on Ted and Pam Ritchie, he being adjutant of this school and an old pal of John's in the Suffolks.

I move over to my quarters today, the Mess being open and some chaps arrived, though the course doesn't start until 3rd April. A letter from Hugh and Peggy and one from Marjorie, being pretty affectionate. I spend a lot of the time swimming, which is good sport, being a natural pool, and no chlorine in it.

April 6th 1940
PACHMARHI

SATURDAYS ARE HOLIDAYS, instead of Thursdays. Interesting work it is, although unfortunately I don't know all the parrot stuff in Urdu; or English for that matter. In the afternoon I write my notes, and then go and play tennis in the Club. After that a drink, come back and change, then I seem to be back there again, on the booze.

A lot of temporary soldiers on this course, and they are good chaps, although some are as old as 34, married with a family, and all on a 2nd Lt's pay. I go to Government House the other day for tea and tennis, most enjoyable, though I enter by the Governor's private gate and drive, and the ADC O'Neill tells me off.

April 20th 1940
PACHMARHI

DOING PLENTY OF WORK HERE. Up at seven, at it from 8.30 until lunchtime. I then relax for an hour or so, have tea and go off to tennis. We have all fallen into our groups and cliques now. I am in one with Roger Green, Dudley Withers RAF, "Lord" Page, R. Berko and mixed up Mulhollands, Ox & Bucks, Retherwick Skins etc. We call ourselves 'the snakes', though Basil Henson[1] is my idea of one.

I am getting browned off with the social side, and saw my club bill the other day, so am laying off for a bit. I am now the underwater expert at Beedam, and last time crossed and re-crossed in one. They call me "Dornford-Yates" – it was "Sulky" with the Wilts. The course is interesting but confusing in the facts accumulated. I sleep very well here, out on the verandah, though storms get up occasionally.. I wish I had a gun. Adams, 2/19, has got a panther and a sambhar. One Pughe, Kings Own, went up for his medical for the RAF and is now told to report to Hamble, near Southampton, on 13th May. God! A letter from Bill, just up from Cairo, and even in the Middle East they have the "Journey's End" atmosphere, and plenty of fun with the nursing sisters, or so he says. Mac Bradley and Gillam 2/7 on this course. I have a 1/500 H.S. burn[2] and some neat H.S. on the other arm. Neat H.S. removed with ointment. I win the plate-lifting at Beedam – money for jam!

[1] *Basil Henson later became a well known stage and screen actor in the UK).*
[2] *A mustard gas -'Hun Stuff' - burn, a result of the chemical warfare training he was undergoing.*

April 29th 1940

SRINAGAR

I ARRANGE TO COME UP ON TEN DAYS LEAVE with Dudley Withers to Kashmir, and so write to Marjorie to fix us up with a boat, and here we are in Srinagar. After the final exam we depart the 25th for Lahore, where his squadron was (now Peshawar) and where his car is. I send Attam Khan on leave and we go to Faletti's for a night. We go to the RAF Mess, purchase a few things in town and go to the cinema. We leave Lahore 28th at 7.30 am and arrive

"En route to Kashmir".

here twelve hours later, having done 320 miles – at least Dudley did – climbing turns from Jammu to Banni Hal, then gliding turns all the way down.

Beautiful scenery all the way, and at about 8700 feet we had to help clear away a landslide. A few snow drifts remaining on the Banni Hal pass. Country very reminiscent of Scotland and, in parts, of the Razmak area.

We go straight to Nedou's for a beer and a clean up, and then take a shikhara to the Buller's houseboat on Dal Lake. I receive a surprisingly warm welcome from the hen and cock Buller, and they have arranged for us to have a boat next door at 5/8 a day each. They give us dinner the first night, and Marjorie has baked us a cake. All very nice and very kind of them. We had asked Marjorie to tea to eat her new cake and she said she would be along. Then at 16.23 comes a chit from Henry Buller saying "Thanks very much for inviting M. to tea but you will remember that in Madras she was never allowed into a chummery[1] and I cannot relax that rule here." Our houseboats are not touching but about three feet apart. Slightly staggered!

This morning I wake up feeling grand, and we go and look at Srinagar and the "Bund", which reminds me of the "seaside" at home, with touts everywhere. We then go and look at Nagin Bag, which is where we wanted our boat originally. The Club annexe is there, and swimming, and not a dirty backwater like our mooring here. Dudley meets some friends there and everything looks rosy, if only we can get away from here without giving offence to the Bullers. I use my catapult on the peddlers and hawkers. Ma sent me out two pipes and a cigarette case, silver with my crest on. Her great scheme of defeating the customs (marking them as repairs) failed, and I have to pay 11/- on the parcel. It was damn hot in Lahore. Our houseboat is called 'Lighthouse'.

[1] *A bachelor pad.*

'The Good Ship "Lighthouse"'. The 'chummery' referred to by Marjorie's father, Henry Buller.

May 2nd 1940

SRINAGAR

WE MANAGE TO GET AWAY TO NAGIN BAGH, and whilst in the Club a girl comes in and we send her a chit from Joan Strallan, who we had brought up with us. We hear it being opened and find that we have struck lucky. She is Elaine Doran, up here with her Ma in houseboat "Butterfly", and is a really beautiful English girl; all her own beauty too, just out from home in January and completely unspoiled. We fix up a picnic with them but rain stops that. We take her to the flics the next day. Yesterday we go into town with the Adams's, Dudley's friends, and then on return play gramophones on "Butterfly" with tea and games with the Adams's. A dance last night at Nedou's and we go there with Elaine and Ma. I get left a bit longer than pleasant with Ma, but still. A wire from Wana extending my leave up to June 9th, or six weeks, so presumably I shan't get any more this year. Oh, Elaine! Met Valentine up here.

119

'Elaine'

May 7th 1940

SRINAGAR

WE BOTH FALL IN LOVE WITH ELAINE and take her out every day. We drive into Srinagar some mornings, go to a dance at Nedou's and the Club and the pictures – something every day. John Palmer

Elaine and Colin on a shikhara on Dal Lake

and wife up here, and we all go to call on them yesterday evening. I saw him in the Club. Met Matthew up here too. Nagin Bagh really is a beautiful place, whether it be wet or fine. It is a curious situation with Elaine. We both go out with her, and I suppose my eyes look to Dudley what his look to me, when looking at her. However I am the junior partner, and she prefers him I think. Mother is a colossal snob, despite her place of origin being Putney, and Pa, who is not here, is reputed to be like the Big Bad Wolf. They reckon to go up to Gulmarg in June for three months, and leave Kashmir in September or October.

I haven't seen Marjorie again – nor do I want to after Elaine. I fall off 'Butterfly' yesterday morning and lose my watch in about 5 feet of pani *(water)*. I go round the boat, diving, this morning but there is too much mud and I can't find it. I've made a catapult for the local bumboat man.

The thought of leaving Elaine is beginning to hurt somewhat but I think it would be better to go to Assam than to stop here, though if I had the clothing etc I might go for a trek. But then I would probably put my foot in it, like I usually do. I don't expect I will get the railway warrants in time anyway.

We have another 'sticky' tea in the Club at Srinagar, but it's not such a success as the first one.

May 14th 1940

Assam

OUR LAST DAY WE WENT UP TO GULMARG with food. I am a bit sore in calf, through falling off the footplate of 'Butterfly', and I have a spirited horse. I get him under control on the way down though. On return we have dinner on 'Butterfly' and go to a dance at Nedou's – coming back pretty grim, and there seems to be something between Elaine and Dudley, which rather worries me. However, such is life. In bed at 3 am and up at 5.30 and we drive off to Pindi, a bloody journey via Murree with two punctures, and we are both rather remorseful. I spend the night at Pindi station with some free beers in the Club where I get in a circle with Robinson 3/10 and some friends of his. Change at Lahore and reach Calcutta on 12th in the morning. I get blackmailed over my excess baggage by the Babu, helped by a YMCA chap, and it costs me 10/-. A helluva job to cash a cheque at the Great Eastern, but after much telephoning of Uncle Stanley's friends I get it backed. *(He is on his way to stay with his uncle, Stanley Wood, a tea planter in Assam).*

Dinner on the Assam Mail, breakfast crossing the Bramaputra on a ferry from Amingoan. Then up through some real African jungle with the cicadas in full throat to Titabar station. Some pleasant shooting out of the train in the morning with my Colt, at Paddy and wading birds, including a stork. Not far out either. Pass a beautiful train smash, with telescoped vans, torn rails and an engine with a really drunken list. The Uncle meets me at the station

*'Panbarry.' The tea planter's house in Assam where Colin's Uncle
Stanley(Stanley Wood) lived. Colin visited twice, in May and December 1940.*

and here I am. Uncle Bill is dead, I am told, and left me £200. Hugh
(Colin's brother) put up a good show and hoping for a DFC. I'm
sure I'll never see this war!

May 18th 1940

ASSAM

THIS IS UNFORTUNATELY A CULTIVATED PART of Assam, the
nearest jungle being 40-50 miles away. However, I go round with
my revolver and a Greener .310 of Uncle Stanley's to see what I can
get. I fail dismally with the .310 as I cannot zero it properly, not that
there is anything worth shooting. Some duck-like wading birds,
king crows, crow pheasants, crows and a bastard cuckoo which says
'Who are you?' the whole time. I spend half a day chasing some

123

jungle fowl. I do a quick draw when I flush them, and one squats on a tree near the .310 but I miss him. However, I shall persevere.

There is a half-eyed pony which I ride a bit. An Australian whaler, and his good eye is damn bad, so that he stumbles and walks into obstacles.

An enervating place this. Breakfast at 9.30 and I don't feel like rising much before. The green is a good sight, and very unlike the India I know. We go over to the Jorhat Club for tennis and tea. I see the AVLH *(Assam Valley Light Horse)* doing their stuff, but was only introduced to one or two. I suppose I am better off than an assistant tea planter on Rs 250/-. This is a peaceful life, and a pity there isn't jungle nearby. An ever still, rising and falling cadence of bird calls. All varieties, the crow and 'Who're you?' predominating. And me out of the war! God!

May 25th 1940

Assam

FORTY EIGHT HOURS STEADY RAIN. Nothing to do. Yesterday managed to bag a cormorant, 'Who're you?' and parrot with the .22. It seems to shoot high according to the sights, so it's all a question of aiming lower by so much and holding her steady. Wrote to Elaine and Joan Strallan. Also to Mowbray Burnett.

The drill here is, rise at 8.30 and then stroll around outside before breakfast at 9.30, of all hours. After the 10.15 news I either go out with the Uncle walking round the tea, or by myself with the Colt. Back at about 12 to read the paper and have a drink. After lunch read, write or sleep until tea at 3.30. After that, shoot or muck about until beer and news at 7.00 pm – and so to bed.

What a life! Forever mucking about is how my life seems to have been spent. Letter from Jobber Benbow, wanting to transfer to 2/13.

May 30th 1940

WENT OVER TO THE MARIANI CLUB and watched the AVLH at drill. Worse than a school OTC. There I observed one Lance Corporal and wondered whether I had come out on the boat with him. Two days later, while dozing on my bed after lunch, I get to thinking about the old days, and eventually about Skegness. I suddenly remember that Thom Allen used to plant tea in Assam, so I nip out of bed and look in the Assam directory. I see an Allan, P living near here and remembering Peter, I enquire off the Uncle. He tells me that he has a brother called Tom who used to plant here, and also that he is the Lance Corporal I had spied. This is too much evidence, and it turns out to be Peter Allan, after fifteen years, and he had been eyeing me too, he said.

Went over to the Government Tea Research Department at Tocklai and there one Benton, bacteriologist, tells me that to purify water, insert two rupees a third of an inch apart, as poles, and then a current through them from a 4.5 volt battery will purify one pint of water in 15 seconds. Provided there is no clay in the pani (water), which combines with the silver and falls to the bottom. I get my hands on a car after three years since I last drove. It's a 1929 Chevrolet. Some good coot shooting, and have opened up on a jackal.

June 7th 1940

WE GO TO THE MARIANI CLUB on Saturday 1st and then I go off for a night with Peter Allan, and what a night. Tennis, a drink and change, then a game of pools, some bridge, and then boozing in the bar with a chap who knew John Macneil, and we leave at midnight. Finish dinner at 2 am, and so to bed. In the Club I had retired at about 10 pm, and after that got my second wind OK.

The next day, tennis with the Butters and back home. We discuss Allan family history since I left them, and this and that. I push off to Calcutta on 3rd, and spend the 4th in the Grand Hotel (12/8). I go out to Dum Dum aerodrome, and am allowed up dual, which I manage OK. The next morning I go out solo, but a damn Indian smashes his undercarriage the turn before me, so no more flying. That being so, I push off to Lahore where I am now, in Falletti's hotel (signed into the book as "Marmaduke, Undertaker").

4th June a memorable day, for that night I discover a secret of nearly nine years standing, though I admit I had overestimated it. Enough said!

A bloody journey on the Punjab Mail, though met one Gilroy (ex 53rd), now AIRO in RIASC. Arrive here at 7.00 am and breakfast and off up to the aerodrome. After twenty five minutes dual, am allowed solo, and just circle and land, though a bit bumpy. I'm fed up with doing landing circuits for ever. Still, it certainly is an expensive hobby, and I can't see what good is going to come out of it ever.

Met Appleton, joining the RAF in Calcutta. Up again this evening for forty minutes. Walters, the pilot instructor, unable to teach me aerobatics, so I go on a recce over Lahore, about ten miles away. Keep at 2000 feet and try to take a couple of photographs. A bit of a haze and much smoke, but most enjoyable, and finish with a perfect landing. The damn man won't let me spin her, me who has spun at 3000 feet in Madras – he says he doesn't like chaps of only six or seven hours flying throwing the planes about. What the hell's he think I am? Met a flying British officer there, and was telling him what Adams had told me about Haig going to the RAF, and found he WAS Haig, and that they had accepted him and then done nothing more about it.

June 16th 1940

I leave Lahore on the Frontier Mail and meet Attam Khan in Lalamusa, where I have to spend quite some time. Arrive at Darya Khan at 4.15am, and then by car to DIK. This entails a trans-shipment across the Indus in a launch, which of course goes aground half way across. Met John in the rest house, and with the aid of a chap in the RIASC workshops, we obtain two cars and drive straight up to Mangai the next day. We spend a night here, and after much telephoning for permission, manage to get a seat in an armoured car coming up the next day. Very comfortable, and a good breeze through the open slit.

In Wana, and find that Freeland has gone to District HQ, Guy of 5/13 is the C.O., Willie and Abbo gone off on jobs, Keen at Political, Maitland Jerry on leave, Niven in Razmak with Patiala State Forces. Present are Guy, Golly, Reggie (adjutant), Bill, Arti and Cotterill. Bill departs on leave and gives me the job of Mess secretary, besides C company and Gas officer. I try to get a grip on the work, and wonder how to lecture on gas in Urdu. I have Uncle Stanley's Mauser .430, which he presented to me, though shells are 55/- a hundred. I work bloody hard the first week, but am now feeling rather depressed. Bill and Toby in the war now, and bits of the Indian Army, but how can I ever be? New battalions 7/13 and 8/13 (13 Frontier Force Rifles) being formed, so presumably some British officers will have to go. What a nice thought. Still further from the war would I go.

June 23rd 1940

A still greater blow. Reggie says that I shall have to go to the TB *(Training battalion)* in Abbottabad shortly. This is being expanded, as well as 7/13 and 8/13. That settles the war for me then. Christ! A PAD *(Passive Air Defence)* scheme here. I get the job of AGO and PADO *(PAD Officer)* and it is the nearest to the war we have got. Sitting for one and a half hours one night in a stuffy blacked out Battalion office, played poker with Maxwell and lost, and last night he comes down here and Reggie, Cotterill and I sit down on him. We each have 6/- and Cotterill gets 15/- off him.

Of course in Abbottabad I shall remain a 2nd Lt, and here the boys will all be acting Captains if not Majors. But what to do? It's my own fault for ever coming out here. The Mess lawn is nice and green and I have swum a bit, but it's not too pleasant. This time last year I was enjoying running up Dun.

July 2nd 1940

Wana

NOTHING OF NOTE. I find I am not bad at six-a-side hockey, after my Razmak rink training. Some football, and have got Rangu trained to bring me a Murree beer when I shout to him "My usual!" On an Indian Officers course, which reminds me of Sandhurst, and it prevents me going out on a Brigade day, though they are nothing here. Springheel returned from leave and started boasting to me about Wana in '21.

Due for the T.B. I suppose, this time next week on the convoy, and for how long I wonder. It puts me still further from the War I reckon.

Had dinner in 1/18 Garwalis mess with Miles the other day. Him I met in Nowshara in December '38 when visiting 2/11. Paddy Nugent killed, and Jeffries, and I can't even get a smell of an Italian, let alone a Boche. I seem to be always frustrated. Frustrated to miss that column with Brain & 59th in November 1938, missed Razcol in August '39, then the RAF, and the other day on the Brigade Day, and those RPs where they all caught it but me. Perhaps I am doomed to become a Babu *(a Hindu wise man)*.

A bit of swimming which is pleasant, and from the Brigade garden comes apricots and just now some battered peaches. Grapes in the garden, but pygmies. Some enjoyable bridge the other night with Jolly, Springheel and Smith, 1/18 staff captain. A colossal dust storm, almost a sand storm, arises and for four days visibility is about 1000 feet. Suddenly it shuts down to 200 feet and dust sweeps across the camp, like the rain squalls in Razmak used to. I sleep out for the first time, and wake up under a brown mosquito net. But worth it.

July 11th 1940

WANA

JERRY RETURNED FROM LEAVE having spent it down in Madras, after Pat Turner. No celebration on the 9th *(Colin's 22nd birthday)*. I play in the young soldiers hockey team against the RA, and then Lock and I have a few beers and he comes over for dinner. Had Ken Mules 1/18 up for bridge last Saturday, and Springheel and I bid a small slam, which I play and win. A lot of drinks with one Dowson (Signals), of Western Electric.

Nothing of note ever happens here. Razmak is alive with dead bodies and lead, and Campbell the Resident was shot up and wounded in the arm in his car near Asad Khel. The Worcesters at Razani, and the Suffolks at Razmak, have casualties every day.

A letter from Mowbray Burnett who is in the Gordons in Singapore. I am due for the Training Battalion on the next convoy, in a day or so I expect. I have no guiding aim in life just now. It used to be Urdu, 2/13, the War, my flying license, the RAF – but now I am sunk as far as the RAF goes, and I couldn't be much further from the War in Abbottabad. For twenty years I have dreamt of a war, and now it comes and I cannot take part in it!!

July 14th 1940

Manzai

Now in Manzai. Came down on the convoy two days ago, with ten British officers. We have to sit in the back, as we are too good an aiming mark in the front seats; or so they say. Up to Sra Kanda Narai I stand in the back of my lorry, being the most comfortable position, and then nip into an ambulance which is following and get a good ride the rest of the way. What a place. I try to sleep outside, and am nearly suffocated. Arthur left on the DIK convoy this morning, and I take the 'Heatstroke Express' tomorrow at 6.00 am with Shaw (2/2), Maclean and Collins (1/18). The 3/8 keep a good John Collins here, made by Andy the Madras Khitnagar.

July 18th 1940

Abbottabad

Not a bad journey on the Heatstroke, as the sky was generally overcast, and so not too much sun. A bath at Mari Indus and tea with the Suffolk BORs *(British other ranks)* there. Change at Daud Khel, reached Campbellpore at 2.45 am until 8.00 am, then Taxila and rail head at Havelian. No transport for getting up here, so I have to get a couple of lorries off the RIASC, and had to pay 5/- for one.

This is rather like Kashmir, and there is plenty of rain just now. Dick Shirley (who I met on the 'City of Venice') (the ship Colin came out to India on) is in the next room, on the same job as me. Met Ray and Peggy Palmer in the Club yesterday. Today a session with the dentist, an extremely comfortable one too, and I send a wire to Ma. It's a good looking spot, though not for wartime, and Ray tells me I shall have no chance of using the Mauser around here. What a war!

*'The Heatstroke Express'. So-called because it carried
passengers in open cattle trucks.*

July 27th 1940

ABBOTTABAD

I NOW HAVE A CAR, A TRIUMPH 8HP of about '31 vintage. I
went down with Pat Kenny to look at second hand cars and found
this, which the experts think is OK. Got down from Rs 650 to
Rs 525, and even then the fellow had a hell of a profit. Kenny did
the bargaining, I signed the cheque, having stepped in after Kenny
had refused to go higher than Rs500, and Dick Shirley made me
pay another Rs20 for three months free service. But I reckon my
driving won't do her any good.

On parade at 6.50 to 9.00 am watching jungly chaps right-
turning by numbers, then 10.15 to 11.00 am in the office – bah! –
and one afternoon a week from 5-7 pm, the rest free (unofficially).
That is the sum total of my day's war work. Useful results therefrom
accruing = nil. The 1/8th from Razmak are here, with Walshe, Hall
and some others I used to know. I haven't yet joined the club, and
there's no need to yet. The pool is too dirty for swimming.

August 5th 1940

THE CAR NOT TOO GOOD IN PETROL. The snake tongued salesman said 30-40 miles per gallon. The first two gallons went 20 miles and the next three since have done about 23 miles each. The carburettor needle is wrong.

Henriques and young Fisher killed, and Halliday got an MC, in Egypt. Had drinks with Abbott last night, and he told me stories of the chaps who went home for mountain warfare in Norway. A letter from Bill in an Egyptian desert.

Had to pass a driving test this morning for my bus. Took an '8 anna' police sergeant round the town and back OK.

August 8th 1940

DICK WENT OFF TO HOSPITAL and died on the night of 6/8. He had been ill on and off for three weeks, and it appeared to be stomach trouble. The post mortem said it was an enlarged heart which had choked him. He always was a runner, and I suppose he strained it. It didn't help pushing my car up yon hill either, when I took him, Bill and John Stephenson up to Kelfani, below Tandiane.

Funeral last evening with Gurkha bands. I had the sword and had to place it on the coffin and remove it at appropriate times. It's a pity, as I should be in Peshawar with him by now, as we had tied up to go this weekend.

August 13th 1940

WENT AND HAD A DRINK WITH RAY the other night. Abbo and

Willie expecting to go home any time now. Freeland apparently commanding Razmak. That'll be nice for them. Not feeling too good these days. I seem to be getting fat, and unable to chase a foot or squash ball with as much vigour as formerly. A very sleepy place this, though I don't in the afternoons. A chap called K.A.R. Khan, attached to the Dogras, is apparently going off to Wana to join the boys. I have not joined the club here and seem to manage very well without doing so. Squash in gunners courts, football, a booze in the mess. My first earthquake the other evening. The mess suddenly shook, and the sound of cracking came from the roof, as though a score or so of bearers were chasing cats across it. Pat and I were outside like a cascara tablet *(a laxative)*, but nothing happened and so we returned to our beer in peace.

August 19th 1940

ABBOTTABAD

WENT OFF TO PESHAWAR ON THURSDAY for the weekend. Had some stomach trouble, and car conked out at Attock – this was mended (carburetter) by a lorry driver, and I reach Peshawar Club and hand it over to Ghulam Sarwar. Dudley Withers in Srinagar unfortunately, and I know what he is doing! A chap called Dibben (1/4 GR) turns up, whom I apparently played rugger against at Stowe. Friday the car was mended, and I fix up to go to Landikotal for breakfast on Saturday, and to look at the Khyber Pass. Also saw Major Loreto DDI, and got a man to show me the bazaar. Bathed and drank draught beer in the club. Saturday Dibben and I depart, and at milestone five the car breaks down again. There is a police post nearby and I ring up the garage. Out comes a man, looks at it, says he must go back for new platinum points, and will be just five minutes. I spend the ensuing hour until his return in smoking and throwing stones at frogs. A mad fakir gives us a brace of corn cobs, our only breakfast. Then start off again, but a temperamental piston frightens me and we return to Peshawar.

133

Reggie Malone comes down after lunch and we spend the evening swimming, and then beer on the lawn. Jobber is in Derha Dun with 6/14th. On Sunday we go round the bazaar. The guide is a Turk, of the royal family driven out by the Russians in 1910, and speaking seven or eight languages. We see the money changers, the streets of the leather, goldsmiths, silversmiths and brass workers, and painted birds in cages. We go to the pottery works, the Police Post roof, and the Afridi bazaar. Jews, beggars, locals with rifles strut about.

I set off at 11.30 and at one stop for an hour on the roadside. Here my car is looted of some Punjabi slippers I had bought in the bazaar. Reggie had told me that Peggy Hennessy, of the SS City of Venice, lived in Wah, her father being chief Punjab cement man there, so I stopped in order to arrive for tea there. This I did and found them all in Murree, but was given tea by the bearer, a very civil bloke. The house palatial. The car now gives trouble. I have been nursing it all the way, but it gets fits of not pulling in top gear, being OK in second. This they say is due to bad carburation. I don't know though.

C.A. Blackwell, C.D. Yarrow missing at Dunkirk. Also hear that Peter Petit had his girl, "the Minx", staying out in Mhow when he was there. No second pips until two and a quarter years service or eighteen months of war, whichever first. Three more months to do for me.

August 25th 1940

ABBOTTABAD

LETTER FROM UNCLE GEORGE DATED JULY 12TH sympathising with the loss of Hugh. *(His elder brother, flying Blenheims for 21 Squadron, went missing over France on 6th June).* First I knew of it, and he doesn't make it clear whether killed or missing. I wire Ma, but I suppose one can't expect an answer these days. I must have done it by what I said to Bill in my letter – tempting fortune

134

though it was too late then. And me sitting here watching 'Ek do tin, nama, ek dot tin'! (A popular local dance, 'One, two, three, let's dance!') God!

Letter from Dudley Withers and as he states "after two days I got so browned off with her dumbness and her foolish mother that I have broken off relations". Fancy that now!

A helluva walk with John Stephenson last night, three and a half hours, and back at 8.15. Peggy says the boys expect to go out on column in Wana shortly. Russell T.S. and Morgan Wall killed the other day, the former at Tabbi and the latter in Razani. Wish I was there, and not here. Managed to get off a letter to Aunt Molly, for my sins. Am due for a trip to Nasirabad with a draft for 7/13.

September 5th 1940

ABBOTTABAD

SET OFF FOR NASIRABAD ON 30TH. Took over train, but my lilo was punctured of course, and with John Stephenson I set off. Parted company at Lahore, where he went on to Solon. Got onto the metre gauge railway at Bhatinda and nearly shook my guts out. Fed very well on a tin or two a day with bread, fruit from the stations and pinky pani (potassium permanganate water solution used to wash fruit and vegetables in). Passed through Ajmer, a big railway colony, and looking prosperous with a car practically at every door. Keith Dawson objected to the boys arriving with their feet out of the windows, and on arrival Pinsent Q/M gave me a sort of operation order for unloading, which I promptly forgot and do no more about.

Lunch with the Dawsons, a bit drunken, and me trying to get a word in here and there. Sleep, walk and booze with Hugh Easton and Pat Thompson 2/11, ex Razmak, with their new battalion there. Bridge with Bill, Springheel who is making a nuisance of himself here, and Felix Williams, and I come back on Sunday arriving here on Tuesday night after a bloody journey. Nasirabad was evacuated in May owing to a water shortage, but now they have returned as it rained a lot recently. Expect to go to Bannu shortly, and relieve 1/12 who are due for mechanisation. Akhbar of 6/13 there. He said we had been going to invade Persia with that force and seize the oilfields, but now not, so expect 59th have gone to Egypt.

Rumours of the boys moving from Wana to Jallundur or Ambala shortly – what the hell will they do there? Sikhs in C.I.H. *(Central India Horse regiment)* refused to embark at Bombay for overseas, so half a dozen of them were shot by court-martial sentence. One transported for fifteen years, but not dismissed the service, so presumably will return on completion.

Abbottabad as bloody as ever, and depression gets worse. Kitty Cole gets married to a Captain Desmond Verney.

September 12th 1940

Abbottabad

Letter from Ma saying Hugh missing on 11th June. "He went on a raid in his Blenheim, the most glorious hot day and though no fighter was after him, he was under fearful A.A. barrage and went up to 7000 feet and was seen no more – " Peggy *(his brother Hugh's new wife)* produces a daughter some few days ago too.

I work in Brigade now, two or three days, as the battalion out training, an interesting interlude, what with all the secret stuff and seeing how things work. It's getting cold here now and depression, mental and physical, is setting in. I don't seem very fit these days, I must say, and nothing ever happens, one day succeeding another. And Hugh.

September 26th 1940

NOTHING OF NOTE. Letter from Tony Cotterill, Wana getting sniped, and the other day six B.O.'s and three orderlies out exercising hounds were ambushed by thirty Dushmen at 200 feetrange. Two horses were hit and the remainder missed. However, Arthur Murray and an orderly fell off in the general confusion and their horses bolt for home, and Mike Oliver apparently rode back in the face of the advancing tribesmen and rescued Doc Murray. Or that's the story anyway. It was a trap to draw out Wanacol where a lashkar was waiting for it. However, the bait was not swallowed. Only some armoured cars went out in pursuit, and the R.A. opened up rapid fire from the camp. Why do I always miss the fun? Campbell apparently can't quite understand life there, and when the gunners opened rapid he was having one of his reports debated before the C.O. The guns started and Campbell interrupts the C.O. with "My God sir, artillery!"

These recruits here are a mixed lot. Some of the Sikhs that arrive speak pretty good English, some have been impressed, some are Nai Sikhs[1], and then some desert after they have been here some weeks. The Dogras are mostly pretty good, and give no trouble at all. Kumaonis we take now, and they are proud and conceited. (A people from northern India). Some have been told to ask for Ghurka hats like the Dogras, and some speak no Kumaon tongue. PMs are alright, some madder than others, but the real madness are the Pathans, especially the Orakzais (A tribe from the North West frontier), with whom no other brand of Pathan is able to converse. There are eight training groups, they spend fifteen working days in each, and then know how to fire a rifle and salute, a bit of V.B., and elementary collective training and mountain warfare.

[1] *A caste of Sikh working in the haircutting or beauty profession.*

October 17th 1940

HUGH STILL MISSING. Nothing of note for a month now. I just live and eat and sleep – or seem to. Saw David Cole get married the other day. There won't be many girls left when I get home, if I ever do. A bit of bridge with Rosemary Abbott, though she can't really play. Abbo' is now at home (Willie too) having gone on a course at Minley. Now cracking with the Pashto, and not finding it too easy. Three months I've been here now, and don't see how I am ever going to get out of it. I tried for 59th, wrote to Brain once or twice, but nothing could be done as they have now gone off to Egypt.

Part 3

RAF training

Karachi

October 28th 1940

IN SEPTEMBER I WAS TALKING to some of the boys from 6 Gurkha Rifles and they mentioned a request for applicants for the RAF. I pricked up my ears and being unable to find it in our office, I went down to the 6/GR office and took a copy of theirs. It read "Suitable BCOs and ICOs wanted for secondment to the RAF – under 28 and with at least 1.5 years service. Previous flying service is not necessary but will be taken into consideration." I sent off a wire to Wana asking permission and then the TB sent up my name. At last, on 26th September, just as I was going down the Mess steps, thinking of Tony Cotterill's letter about the ambush, and how I always miss everything, an orderly arrives with this telegram: "2nd Lt D-W provisionally selected for secondment RAF – will be required to commence initial training about end September. Should be warned accordingly. Further instructions will issue shortly."

I am overjoyed, start packing and get drunk. I then get more depressed as the days go on, and eventually a wire comes on 25th October saying report Air H/Q for medical on the 28th. If pass, then off to Karachi for training!

I come down with Bobbie Elsmie, off to Bombay to be married, and Logan Gates, whose wife and daughter died the other day (I attend funeral). I stay here in the Cecil and go round to drink with Brain, who is now a military secretary here.

This morning I roll up at Air H/Q and meet Haig (5/19), Pringle (2/10) and Gillespie (1/10), all pilots bar the latter. We hang about for hours for our medical and interview by Group Captain Bussell. Major A.S. Lewis (4/12) is Air Liaison Officer and does all the paperwork.

I mention my eyes and they all look grave. I am walking around the quad, looking at the pretty typists (it's the Nizam of Hyderabad's palace) when I see the M.O.'s room and Haig on his exam – I also see the eye test board, so I write it down, (it seems to be a gift – "never look a gift horse in the mouth" etc.), memorise it, and am passed as 6/6. How long it will last I don't know. I reckon I will be pushed out after a few weeks, or even days, but it will be good fun whilst it lasts.[1]

Our course is six weeks at Drigh Road, Karachi, then 4 Air Training School Iraq, and back to Army co-operation squadrons in India. Rank Pilot Officer, pay Army or RAF, whichever is the higher. After a year we go into RAF uniform. Off tonight on the Frontier Mail to Lahore and then on to Karachi – the great deceit – how long will it last – and will I be court-marshalled – Quien Sabe?

[1] *Colin's eyesight was poor, and he expected to be found out eventually.*

November 2nd 1940

KARACHI

DRIGH ROAD[1]. We stop at Lahore for the day on the way down. Pringle and Haig went to see the Flying Instructor there, Walters. Gillespie and I sit about Faletti's and go for a swim out in the Cautt. Then down on the Sind Express, plenty of dust and no restaurant car. We ride a bit in the engine compartment – rushing through the night down south – arrive Drigh Road at 8.00 pm – met by a three-ton lorry and taken to Mess – filled with beer by F/Lt J. Chapple, Adjutant. We live in tents here, of the marquee type with concrete floor, a water point, and an electric punkah overhead. I open up at night and such a breeze comes blowing through that I can sleep with a blanket on. As "Red Hot" Jones, the civil flying instructor, is away, we spend about five days hanging about the works and watching things happen.

The depot here repairs all crashes, assembles planes shipped from home, and now that not so much is coming out, it is a factory for all sorts of engine parts. It's in the desert seven miles from

141

Karachi – a nice Mess, but rather regimental in its rules and with notices everywhere saying "such and such is verboten" etc. We couldn't get dinner at 10.00 pm the other night!

Went to the boat club for a swim the other day, it's on a creek of the Chinna and a pleasant spot. Bond is here, but mad, and doesn't take much stock of me. Dudley Withers arrived here suddenly two days ago, as Armament Officer for six months, whatever that is. He flew a Wapiti *(Westland Wapiti)* down from Peshawar. Well, we both went into town for one, and sat in the Boat Club for a few hours, exchanging talk and reminiscences. It was just like the good old days on Nagim Bagh, with Karachi all blacked out, looking like the other side of Nagim. We then called in at the Gym Club and had another.

Dicky Lonsdale, Leicesters, awarded MC for Waziristan – Razmak I suppose. Johnny Benbow's engagement in the paper! Christ! is the only suitable comment. Well, I've been about four days in the RAF now – pretty good going eh?

---

[1] *The four Indian Army officers are accepted for secondment to the RAF. In total, 60 were transferred under this scheme. The Air Ministry gazetted them as Pilot Officers attached to 'General Duties Branch, RAF' in the London Gazette (30/10/41), service numbers 47299 (Haig), 47300 (Pringle), 47301 (Gillespy) and 47302 (Dunford Wood). They are posted together to the 4th Intermediate Flying Training School at RAF Habbaniya in Iraq.*

November 8th 1940

KARACHI

'RED HOT" JONES GOT BACK MONDAY, so we have done four days flying since then. Circuits and landings and ten minutes solo the last two days. I get in a bit of side slipping for the first time. Jones takes us in a DH60 but he doesn't wear earphones, and you can't always understand him. Ground work, theory of flight and we learn to 'buzz' up there. We have a go in the "Link" (trainer) too – a beautiful toy. At 1000 feet all you can see is desert, with the sea

Tiger Moths at the Karachi Flying Club.

eastwards, not at all a bad sight. Went out fishing on Sunday, with
Jones, Bowden and Dudley in a sort of dhow. Out past Manora and
I was sick – caught the only fish, but too ill even to haul it up. It's
easy to sit here and say how nice the sea is, and how I would like
to experience a real rough storm, but it's bloody hell when you get
there.

We go up to the aerodrome at 7.30 every day, and back at
about 1 pm. We live in a sort of Ipi hut, with canvas sides and a
thatch roof to keep the sun off the canvas. At night I open her up to
a decent breeze and sleep with a blanket on. Jock McGrath collects
a DFC at home, and has his picture in the "Sketch"! The beer tastes
nice here, the old Murree!

November 11th 1940

KARACHI

HAD THE FIRST GAME OF RUGBY SINCE "BLIGHTY" the other
day – didn't manage too badly, except for having bars in my boots

LICENCE 3.				LICENCE 4.
		RENEWAL OF LICENCE.		
	Medical Examinations.		Periods of validity of Licence.	

Date.	Result.	From	To	Signature (or stamp) of responsible officer.
16.11.39	Fit subject to wearing correction to vision.	18.3.40	15.11.40	
18.11.40	Fit	22-11-40	17-11-1941	

and so unable to move. It is played on the mud flats here, quite softish, though I cut my knees a bit. Went out with Gillespie in the desert yesterday evening and I shoot a hare and a partridge – there's some sand grouse about, though out of range. A hell of a wind today, and I do three bad landings, Gogte using the engine each time to save the undercarriage. Hope I'm better tomorrow.

November 13th 1940

KARACHI

GOT THE LANDINGS TAPED – I had been flattening out too late. Did two hours solo yesterday and today. This morning went out to a village on the creek due east and then climbed to 8000 feet – it was damn cold, so I came down, doing a bit of side slipping. This evening we go up and I had prepared a trip to Hawk's Bay. But I have a preliminary chukka and during the landing, I seem to be going too damn fast. Well, I bounce four times, get my tail up, damage the undercarriage slightly, and take three inches off the

144

airscrew. Jones is not too annoyed, and eventually takes me up in the Tiger and shows me when to use my engine. Though I really knew all along.

Yesterday went to the Boat Club after dinner. Saw P. Bond and talked of this and that. Met one Hayes, who succeeded me in ULIA attachment to Leicesters, and is now in the Baluchi Training Battalion here. Also MacDowall, who is an acting major in 7th GR. And as conceited as hell. I only talk to him for about ten minutes but I am nearly sick! Damn me for a B.F. this evening!

November 18th 1940

Karachi

NEARLY SCUPPERED. As my 'A' License expired on 15th inst. I had to have a medical exam for the renewal form. Crimes of Paris! As the saying goes.

Well, I go snooping around the hospital on the pretext of getting some boric ointment, but am unable to penetrate the medical officer's section and obtain access to the eye test card. So I nip down to the RAMC Hospital on Sunday morning. The C.O. there is a bit deaf and says 'come tomorrow at 9.00 am', I explain that I shall be flying, but he just repeats himself. I then see one Captain Hanbury on the list of doctors (he was at Pachmari) so I chase him around the wards, but unsuccessfully.

I then run into the C.O. again who is a bit rude, so I pack off home. I go straight up to the hospital here with my heart in my boots, but the M.O. is out. However, I penetrate his office and write down the eye test card, which is C-O-O etc in unfinished circles. I learn this off by heart, and this morning I go up for the inspection. He is in one of the wards, and as he fills in the questions he says "Come along with me and I'll test your eyes." He leads me out of the ward but PAST his office, and I hear the angels singing. We then come to a placard on the wall, and damn my whiskers if it isn't the same one as I learnt in Delhi at Air HQ!

Well, I learned RAF climbing turns etc, and can now do steep turns and side slips. There's a small camp some 3-4 miles from the aerodrome, presumably Kings Own, and I do all my stuff there at 4000' and then shoot them up in the remaining 3000' to 1000' after which I go home.

A dance in the Mess here last Saturday. McDowell rings up and invites himself, with a colossal fat chap in Phipson's called Connie. He wants to come as all the "Popsies" are here and he wants to get amongst 'em. Suits me. I have a few dances, nothing much to write home about, and eventually retire at 02.30.

November 21st 1940
KARACHI

FLYING MORNING AND NIGHT. Went off solo in the Tiger (Moth) for an hour yesterday, and was surprised how well I got on. Yesterday Jones taught us loops, and today I go up for an hour and did fifteen of them, a spin, and half a dozen stall turns; I did one, and only lost 400'.

After I had flown the Tiger yesterday, "Red Hot" forgot to see how much petrol was left, and did a forced landing 400' off the aerodrome, in spite of his 12,000 hours flying. He gets into his cockpit with a little black bag every morning which, we have now discovered, contains his breakfast. This he has in the air when he has given it "over to you". Someone crudely suggested that he didn't only have breakfast up there.

December 1st 1940
KARACHI

WELL, "RED HOT" HAS SHOWN US LOOPS, rolls and half rolls, but apart from loops, the others get worse every time I practise them. I'm flying the Tiger quite a lot, but even so, these bloody rolls are the bane of my life. The other day Jones produces his Rocket Loop, and bloody well blacks me out for half a second or so. Not my idea of fun at all.

I have now been to Hyderabad solo and dual cross country, and there's nothing much in it. Interesting the first time there, but that's all.

A letter from Air H/Q that we leave on January 7th. Well I have about three hours of my solo left to do, the others the same, so Jones has written off to try and get us some more flying. The buzzing is progressing *(radio comms),* though I send better than I receive it.

Went to visit Mac the other day. Edward Hill is Adjutant. I nearly starve at dinner, but his Indian can feed five hundred with a couple of loaves and a fish!

Am slowly getting the mastery of the "Link"[1] and we are now dabbling in Lorentz approaches – though what bloody good that will ever be to us, I don't know.

Two letters from Bill, who seems to be working pretty hard, but doesn't say whether he has been in action yet or not. Reading Compton Mackenzie's 'Four Winds of Love' which makes life seem sort of peaceful.

[1] *A series of flight simulators produced from the early '30s by Ed Link, based on technology he pioneered in 1929 in New York. They were a key pilot training aid.*

December 9th 1940
KARACHI

MY SLOW ROLLS GET WORSE AND WORSE – I stick on my back and even Jones can't see why. My knee gets jammed up against the petrol pump by the stick at times, when she is right over to the right, and I don't think that helps much. Have half an hour solo, about two hours dual and two hours 'Link' left to do. Extra flying not sanctioned, so we are recommended to apply for about fourteen days leave and come back a week before we sail. Where the hell shall I go.

Went out shooting to Kalri near Tatta where there are three or four large jhils. (Hindi: shallow lake). Went on Saturday with Ian Pringle, S/Ldr Bowditch and one Evans, and their wives. We stayed in the PWD (Public Works Department) rest house, and had food laid on by the Mess and cooked by my bearer. Popsie Crick laid on the banda but then got malaria, so he could not come. Hid in a hide for duck on Saturday night, and got two for twenty-three cartridges, and lost one of those. Shocking shooting, but magnificent opportunities.

Then shot all Sunday morning and I got a duck and five snipe, two of which were lost. Driven snipe – bloody hard. A lovely place I'd like to go back to, and smoke and listen to the birds.

Bought a .22 Winchester five-shot the other day for 120/-. Traded my colt for 80/-. I thought he might allow me about 30/- for it, but true to character I asked 100/- and he just mildly expressed that it was a little high. I was then so taken aback, when asked for another figure, I was foxed, but managed to get out 70/-. Suleiman Omer, the gunsmith, then jumped at this so I said I would give him 40/- for the rifle – and there the deal closed. Unfortunately its spring American peep sight is U/S *(unserviceable)* and is only sighted up to about fifty yards. Though I have not really zeroed it yet.

Pete Gillespie is in my tent now as accommodation is scarce. We got talking last Sunday. I mentioned aims in life, one thing turned to another, and I discover he tried to desert when war broke out, and get home and join up. Got to Bombay and the only ship he could find was American, and the captain offered to take him to the States. However, he thought he'd rather go the other way, but was unable to find a ship that would take him. His money then ran out, and just as he thought of going to Goa, he couldn't do it, so surrendered to the SSO. Was court marshalled as AWOL and sentenced to six months loss of seniority. A bloody good effort I call it. He also passes bouncing cheques, without malice aforethought he assures me. But that's another person who thinks of life the same way as I do. The Gurkha in Pachmari was the other.

Went out with Dudley for a few drinks in the Gym Club the other day after dinner. We then came back and talked for some time in his car, a nearly new Ford 10.

The Aerodrome Officer spotted my "A" License racket, and rang up the M.O. to ask how was it the original license said "Fit (subject to wearing correction of vision)", whilst his form said my eyes were OK. So I rang up the M.O. and explained, laying myself at his mercy, and thank god we came to the conclusion that the aerodrome officer was a bastard, didn't understand good Scots, but was only doing his duty anyhow. Eventually I got it endorsed 'fit' but I bet he's reported it to Delhi, and I suppose that will be my undoing.

I am now wearing two pips[1], being fed up with being asked what I did before the war. I qualified on 26th November, but god knows when it will be through.

[1] He was promoted from 2nd Lieutenant to Lieutenant.

December 20th 1940

Assam

PUT IN FOR TWENTY DAYS LEAVE until 6/1/41 so as I could get to Assam. Sanction never came, but I was allowed to catch the plane on the 18th, and so I may yet be recalled. With 44lb, a suitcase, blanket and the Winchester, we leave before dawn in a Waco (a biplane), AKI Manilal the pilot. After Jacobabad I take her over, and do about 1 1/2 hours to Lahore, where some other passengers get on and cramp our style. Karachi-Calcutta 373/- return. Meals on the Coy I.N.A. In Delhi stayed at the new Imperial (13/-) and in the evening I walk round to the "Circle" for want of a better

149

name to describe it, looking at the shops and wondering if this really is India or not.

The next morning off in a Beechcraft a/c via Cawnpore and Allahabad. The other two passengers get off at Allahabad, and I take her over for three hours then, after Manilal got her through a rain squall. The roof leaks on me, but the pilot reads a book, and I carry on safely at 7000'. These canals are the devil for navigation, as you never know which is the one on your map out of the forty on the ground.

Staying at the Grand (15/-) and last night went to see "Turnabout" and laughed like a drain. Also consolidated my objective again and, knowing the ropes, I got off 15/- cheaper, but is it worth it? Definitely Not.

Hope to God I'm not recalled, but I suppose it's too much to expect. That chap Manilal used to fly Croydon-Paris, and was a curious bird. You can always tell the Indian who has been to England, apart from curry servers in Indian pubs, from the Dera Dun etc product.

December 24th 1940

Assam

HAD A PLEASANT TRIP UP, and breakfast on the Brahmaputra again. Panbarry much the same, only so hot and much damper. Absence of "Who are you?" birds.

The Winchester is going damn well, as by chance I arrived at a position in the screw peep sight which is dead accurate at about 60-70 yards, aim 6 o'clock inner for under that range, and similar adjustment for longer ranges. Hit a paddy bird at 150-200' and also shot a vulture through the neck and down he came. Was inveigled into playing golf with the Ashleys, and saw Peter Allan at the Mariani Club – he remembered about my eyes, the old devil. The doves make a pleasant noise and in fact I should like to live here – but then of course I wouldn't.

December 27th 1940

ON CHRISTMAS EVE HAD A FEW DRINKS with the Kenwoods down the road. Christmas they came here for supper. Uncle Stan opens a bottle of wine, and there is laughter and much ado about nothing.

I spend my time shooting vultures, or so it seems, and they always seem to roost in the same trees, so after learning where the trees are, it's too easy. Yesterday went down to the only patch of jungle round here, a few acres and too thick to penetrate, and shot a monkey, there being no other inhabitants. This morning went out on a vulture parade and observed two jackals eating a vulture's corpse, so shot them on the spot. On finishing them off, I thought their heads didn't quite resemble pukka jacks, and then some Assamese villagers turned out, and I gathered I had shot someone's chowkidars (guard dogs), they wanted 500/- compensation and would fetch a policeman from Jorhat. Though I can't understand Assamese, or the language which the coolies speak – akin to Urdu.

A magnificent sunset yesterday – blood red, orange – and reflected on the Naga hills, which had low-lying fleecy clouds on 'em, and golden ones above. But impossible to describe. Damn cold at night, but the sun is just warming, and no topee required. A pity there's no jungle and big game.

January 5th 1941

KARACHI

I HAD ARRANGED TO LEAVE ON THE 29TH and was just returning to tea on the 28th, after a last dekko at the monkeys (I get into the jungle and slay a couple up trees), when a wire comes from the Aircraft Depot: "Return immediately." I come back at the normal time, after going to Peter Allan for supper on the 28th, and arrive

Delhi on the 31st, having been unable to fly owing to one of INA's directors being on board *(Indian National Airways)*.

I stay at the Great Eastern, good food and a dirty cell for Rs 10/-, then stay at the Cecil, and spend New Year's Eve in my bed with a book. On the 1st, go to Hyderabad House and ask about ranks, pay and why I was recalled. Not known. Also when in Iraq (if reached) do we get RAF pay, British Army with colonial allowance, or Indian Army with overseas allowance? They know nowt of course, but will look into the matter (if they remember). Actually, they were all staggering into each other's offices and saying "Oh I say, Claude – it must have been too many gin and tonics last night – what! – I feel awful."

Next day arrive Karachi, having flown most of the way myself. Manilal again is the pilot – we go to 9000 feet and then fly through and above the clouds, my first experience of them. On asking about this leave, J. Chapple said that the day I left on fourteen days leave, a message comes saying we could only have ten, so they let me have my ten and then recalled me – so I had 15 days in all. Met Dickie Bird in the Mess, from Madras, and we talk about the good old times and "who married who – my god, really?!"

Next day Chapple casually mentions we need passports for Iraq, but "show 'em to me in two days time." We sort out the Iraq consulate from the Afghan and Turk ones, and find we require passports to be valid for Iraq, vaccination certs, an official order detailing us there, and two photographs. We ferret out the passport officer from a mass of City Magistrates and High Court Officers and their clerks' counter directions and find we want another order from the RAF, as all passports are invalid in time of war. Get photographed and return to lunch, exhausted.

That evening Gribbon of the King's Own telephones – "wasn't I at Beacon with him? – yes – then come shooting tomorrow, OK?" (Colin's prep school in Sevenoaks).

He takes me out to Kalri again, where Evans of the King's Own, his Mrs and aged Ma and Pa have been in occupation for ten days or so. I am stuck in the water in a hide at 3.30 and leave it at 7.15 with two ducks and minus twenty-two cartridges.

A very jolly supper, and Nigel Gribbon and I exchange reminiscences well into the night on our beds. Up at six and off to a damn big jhil *(lake)*. The old man, seventy with Boer War medals, and I – he well greatcoated and blanketed – are taken away in a boat one way, the others and the lunch departing north. I shoot a coot with the Winchester on the way for the boatmen to eat, it being duly hallaled first. We maroon Poppa, and I am taken to my hide. I am handed off the boat first and am nearly up to my waist, and so without having got wet himself, the Shikari is able to judge it too deep, and they make me another. Then I am also marooned, the fellow going off to "beat", and promising lunch later.

About 1.00 pm, three hours later, I see Poppa has evacuated his stall and is thawing himself on dry land, so we whistle up the boat and return, with great difficulty, against an icy wind. Great anxiety at the base, and not much lunch left. On swapping notes, we find the boatman did no beating but spent his time cooking my coot under Poppa's blanket. Return to Kalri for tea, with a "spot" in it, and dropped here by Gribbon at 6.00 pm. A great weekend.

January 10th 1941
Karachi

Now the news is in that we embark on the 13th, having been struck off duty on the 17th December. An "Iti" submarine reported off the Indian coast along Persia way, so I hope I don't lose all my baggage.

Letter from Bill in Cyprus – none from Ma since October.

On Tuesday I dined with Nigel Gribbon and then went to the boat club. He then left and I joined a party of the boys including the Simpsons – Mary Simpson – and one Violet, the latter being Alan Haig's fiancée. I am supposed to look like Simon, and his wife

153

'Easy morals at Sandspit.'
Mary, Pete Gillespy and Joan, at Sandspit beach.

Joan spends the whole time pointing this out to people. H.R. Irwin of Mahrattis and one Humphries of 17th have arrived to take over from us, also one Fairweather of 4 Gurkha Rifles. Humphries is banging glasses at this party to see how hard it can be done without them breaking, when quite rightly a neighbour objects, comes over, and they square up and above one another like fighting cocks. Pete then turns on Humphries and gives him no end of a dressing down. They go out for a fight but Haig smooths it over. Bed at 4 am.

Next day off to Sandspit *(famous beach southwest of Karachi)* – Simpsons, Mary, Violet, Pete, Haig and I. I ignore Mary at first, and after some whispering, Joan asks me if I have met her, I say no, and she introduces us. Mary then proceeds to vamp me – successfully, I admit, but most amusing all the same. All day at Sandspit. Bathed but damn cold. Roll on the 13th. I am not taking much kit, as I don't expect to last out long in Habbaniya.

Part 4

4th Intermediate Flying Training School

RAF Habbaniya, Iraq

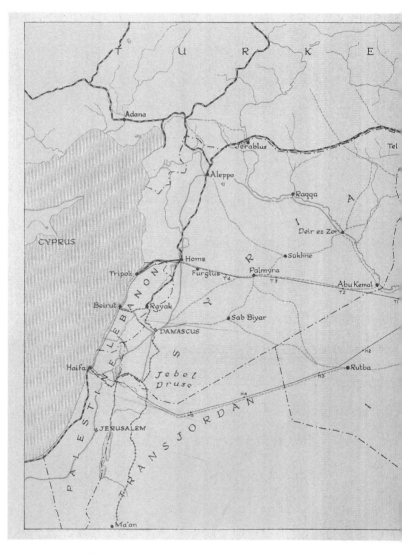

*A map of Iraq, Syria, Palestine, Lebanon and Transjordan in 1941,
showing Habbaniya just to the west of Baghdad, and the railway
running through northern Iraq to Syria.*

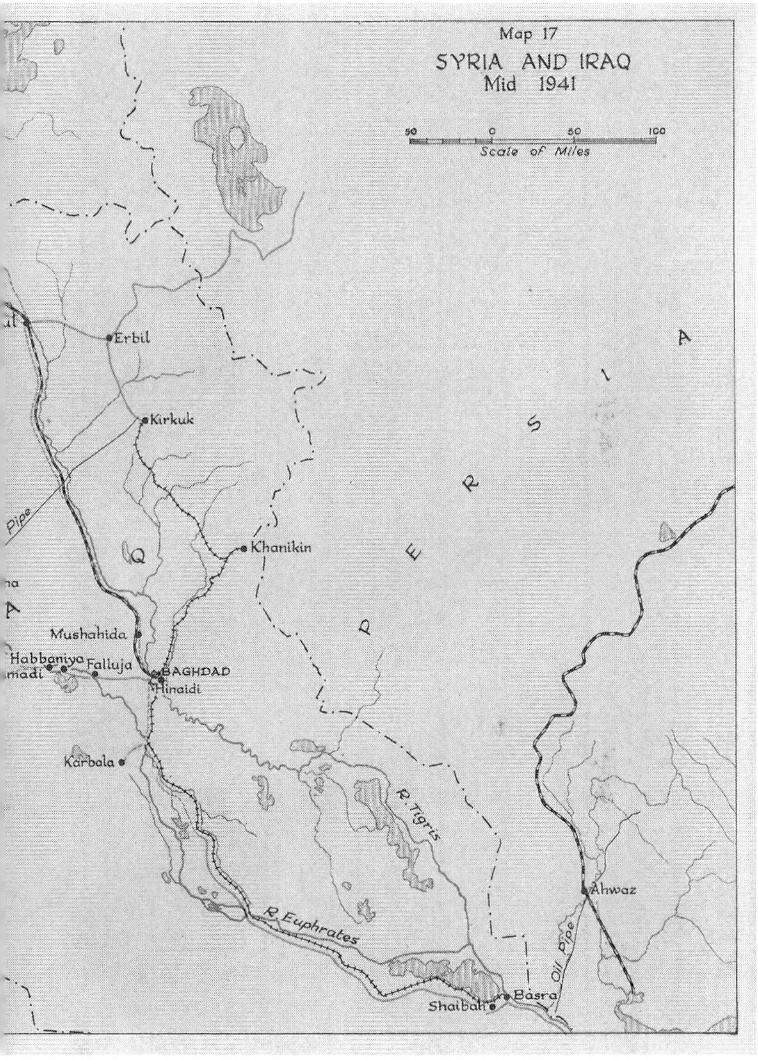

Map 17
SYRIA AND IRAQ
Mid 1941

A line from Kirkuk shows the oil pipeline running to Haditha,
where it splits into the T branch, to supply the French in Tripo-
li, and the H branch, to supply the British in Haifa.

January 14th 1941

At sea

Bed bugs and blackouts...S.S. "Barpeta". A party on the 12th with Pete, Allan, self, Simon, Joan and Mary. A bit low. We go to the boat club and have supper and play the fool. Pete hurdles the chairs and tables and holds Mary upside down so that her knickers become exposed. Low talk by Simonson's concerning bananas. I get Mary on my knee and give her another of my "let me be your father" talks, which are quite good. In bed by 1 am. Irwin, brother of Pat in Madras, was at Delhi some time ago and saw in Hyderabad House (RAF HQ) a list of our eight names, with columns etc – age, regiment, qualifications. It read "A" License for most but by Pete's was "court marshalled for attempting to join the RAF".

We reach the harbour at 9.30 am yesterday after calling at 2 Bath Island Road on the way, and beating the girls under the bedclothes, and embark without fuss or formality. "Barpeta" is 3000' tons, with four other first-class passengers and a lot of deck passengers, and is a "slow" gulf boat. Calls at all the ports, Ormara at 4.00 am this morning, 150 miles from Karachi, and so on. Bed bugs and blackouts...

Out of India at last, but for how long? I suppose I shall be back in Abbottabad in a month or so, or even less, looking a damn fool. We are given thirty days advance pay before we leave. British rates less Indian income tax, so we lose about 200/- on the deal. At Pasmi half a dozen bunderboats descend on us like vultures and fight for places alongside. Bales of Japanese cotton are unloaded by Baluchis and some sort of black Africans. Small boats sell fish, some as long as four feet. Two old Sinbads with beards keep alongside for some hours selling fish, holding the tiller lines between their toes to keep their hands free for paddling. A barren coastline like the Red Sea. Pasmi is a great smuggling port as it's duty-free. The Jap cloth goes to Quetta, duty here being only 18%, whereas in Karachi it's 98%.

January 16th 1941

REPENT SINNERS, FOR THE LORD IS AT HAND. Yesterday called at Charbar in Persia. Mud buildings and forts. Last night big seas get up and I am twice soaked in my bunk before closing the port. A regular "repent sinners for the Lord is at hand" night. Muscat today, a small bay surrounded by Waziristan-like crags with picquets and sangars on them, all painted with the names of visiting ships from 1878 – 1941. Helluva swell on. Negroes come out and dive for coins. This must have been a den of pirates once. Round the corner another town, Muttra, looking through the glasses like an illustration in a book of someone's adventures in the last century. All the ships' boats are out in case we meet that submarine, which is supposed to have cut the Indian cable. A bloody cold wind in this Gulf of Oman. Chess with Pete but cannot beat him –

January 17th 1941

REACHED KUHAWEI THIS MORNING, a small island off Oman Peninsula leased as a naval depot. We land provisions for the R.I.N. sloop present in the bay. Saw some nasty-looking garfish. The Chief Engineer won't tell me a thing, as he says it's all top secret, but had it all from the first mate this afternoon. Now in Bandar Abbas and there's an Italian ship that's been taking refuge here since the war began. A low-lying coastline and a bit of a haze, but it seems a bigger town than any so far.

Two Italian submarines were caught by HMS Falmouth up here some six months or so ago. One was trapped, owing to its rendezvous being discovered in the papers of the captain of the one brought into Aden by a trawler some months ago.

SS Barpeta

January 18th 1941

At sea

LINGAH – AN OLD PERSIAN TOWN and apparently mostly uninhabited. After a long delay, boats come off to the shop and the confusion and noise of mooring and unloading is phenomenal, worse than anything encountered in India, everyone shouting at the top of his voice, and doing his bit of work irrespective of it dovetailing with his neighbours.

January 19th 1941

At sea

BAHRAIN ISLES – WE ALL FOUR GO ASHORE HERE and after purchasing a few things, call on Pringle's friend Dunn, manager of the local bank. We have a beer and then get into a taxi and say "Club". He takes us a twenty-mile drive across the island, through date palms, eventually petering out into desert, covered in mounds, apparently graves. We then reach the oil camp where there is a magnificent, up-to-date club (Bahrain Petroleum Co) with every possible, etc etc. We buy a book of tickets, walk in and meet Scottie Anderson, off the ship, who is going to Saudi Arabia. I have some beers and martinis and then we find it too late for lunch, as his launch leaves at 2.00 pm.

We escort him back and as our own launch goes at 3.00 pm we hang about till then. The shops are rather like Port Said and everywhere are luxurious American cars, not a single old crock being seen. Six yanks come back onto the ship with us, going on vacation to Persia. Quite a social joint apparently, but after the bombs dropped, all the American women were evacuated.

January 22nd 1941

At sea

Spent a day in Bushire in a gale and fog, waiting for the dhows to come off. Eventually cleared and they came out. The Americans gave a party last night and we all go into a cabin – twelve of us. Allan plays his accordion and we all sing, though only with difficulty do we find a song that both "sides" know. It's just like being at the films to listen to these boys.

Went ashore today at Kuwait – an exceedingly clean bazaar, streets swept, very few flies. Almost a free port, only 5% duty. All the inhabitants have queer puckered eyes, as though all afflicted. We see a plane, so hop in a taxi and say "Aeroplane". We find her landed in the desert, a 'Vincent' *(Vickers Vincent biplane)*, and I talk to the pilot, one Geary from Shaibah. We tell him we have been seconded from the army, and he says "Oh yes, airgunners." Airgunners!

161

RAF Habbaniya from the air. Air House (the camp HQ) is the large building midway along the bottom edge, with the polo ground in the bottom right corner.

January 26th 1941

HABBANIYA, IRAQ

MORE DRINKS WITH THE AMERICANS (Joe Carroll) who get off at Al-Khamshah. We land at Basra, are met by an RAF Sergeant and then catch the evening train to Baghdad.[1]

The Customs pinch my .22 and shotgun. Basra is a pretty filthy joint with dim narrow streets, rendered so by the first floor jutting out over the ground-floor shops. I take in my watch for repairs and am told it will be 5/-. When I call later I put down 3/- and the chap says he wants 7/-more. I make it up to 4/- and he is quite satisfied.

We go to the Kit Kat Club and see the cabaret practising. A luxurious corridor train to Baghdad – soap and towels etc, and English-style coaches, but bloody cold in Baghdad. Here we spend two hours until the driver has finished his errands. The main street is like an English country town – thronged with chaps from all over the near and middle east.

The road out here (to Habbaniya) is sixty miles across flat open plain, and twenty miles of nothing, not even road, across Falluja Plain – a pukka sand desert. We are met on arrival and given drinks.

Much drinking last night, and met Garner, who was at Peterborough with Hugh. Dinner at 9.30 and a party at the next table, including Loyd (SWB and Levies), hurling whisky and sodas, plates of butter and pursuing each other over and under the table. Looks like we've come to a madhouse. Shops damn expensive – in Basra, Baghdad and here (25/- for a R10 pair of shoes).

[1] *Harry Hopkins, an advisor to Roosevelt who had recently visited the area, quipped: 'The Persian Gulf is the arsehole of the world and Basra is eighty miles up it.'*

February 2nd 1941

HABBANIYA

HABBANIYA IS A CAMP WELL LAID OUT, rather similar to Wana or Razmak, but vaster and better organised. Training here are a lot of Greeks and South Africans, and they had Norwegians and French before we arrived. We are the only four officers on this course, the rest being other ranks from Kenya and Malaya. We fly Harts, and I have already done four hours and not gone solo, and it looks as though I shall get myself chucked out – which would be the "irony of fate".

Up at 6, flying until 9, breakfast and lectures until 12.30. Then, next day, lectures until 10 and fly until 12.30 – and so on, alternately.

Went racing yesterday, first time since Blighty and on Pete's selection ended 100 fils to the good. A very nice boat club here on Lake Habbaniya, where the flying boats come down, where I went out on a whaler with Charles Braybrookes and some sergeants.

This is the middle of a desert and dust storms make life bloody. The Euphrates runs alongside, and last year the camp was evacuated to the plateau above the lake as there was a danger of the river bursting the bund. Flt Lt Cremin is my instructor and he is nagging and quite contemptuous of my efforts, which doesn't help at all. Saw a drinking game called "Cardinal Puff" yesterday, which is sheer murder by alcoholic poisoning, unless the victim watches his step.

My bearer is a bit of a wag, but not as good as Attam khan (I got him a job with Walker in the Pathans in Wana) – he has a ticket every year in the Irish sweep, and knows a little Urdu thank god. Will I be thrown out? Christ!

February 5th 1941

HABBANIYA

MY INSTRUCTOR IS CREMIN.[1]

First hour or so is spent in my U/S (unserviceable) telephones, with "Br....umph!" coming through them and me feverishly looking at all the bloody dials to see what I am doing wrong. Then I change them and go up with Sgt Baker – do very well, he says "well you know where the bloody ground is anyway!" and that I ought to go solo the next day. Then follows four hours with Cremin and I am bloody awful – he gets my back up with his tired, bored and pained voice: "Must you aim for the only plane on the bloody field?" when I am coming in, and thinking which side to go to avoid a plane on the ground. "Are you doing it on purpose?" when I get into

164

A Hawker Hart trainer

difficulties keeping straight on landing, and the plane continues turning.

Then I go up with Broughton and he shows me how the brakes work. Then Garner takes me up and I improve. Next day, Chief Flying Instructor Squadron Leader Ling gets in the back and I do a perfect circuit and landing, followed by three bad landings. More Garner, but still bad landings. Then Ling says "Well, you know the rules. I've told B flight to give you a couple of hours more" – and then out I go.

Today went up with Garner and did three landings, good enough, and am allowed solo, and do two not-so-bad ones. And that postpones the execution, but I still feel that the sentence has not yet been remitted. Played bridge with C.O. Ling and Broadhurst. Lost 230 fils.

---

[1] *Dan Cremin was killed in an air accident in March 1942 a few weeks after taking command of his first squadron, 66 squadron in the UK.*

February 12th 1941

THE OTHER DAY I WENT UP IN THE CLOUDS and was shown climbing and steep turns. Then up for 1.10h in an Audax to practice. Rain wet the aerodrome, and Harts can't even use the runaways *(runways were known as runaways in 1941)*, as water gets into the brakes and makes them U/S.

Got up today with Garner and I couldn't do climbing and steep turns, and then forgot to circle round before spinning. Why have I become such a B.F.? Did a bit of Duty Pilot, and drew 100 dinars today, advance of some pay or other. Have started learning Arabic, the colloquial variety, and will have a third lesson today I hope. I am introduced to Monopoly.

Nearly 3 1/2 months in RAF, by god. How much more? Whisky is 14 fils a peg.

February 22nd 1941

WENT TO HOSPITAL LAST WEEKEND with the crabs. Shave and put on some strong blue ointment. Now suffering from stubble trouble. Went out sailing in Braybooks's Moth the other day. My first three attempts to 'go about' failed through not letting go of the rudder, but soon mastered that, and had a damned good day.

Flying still going strong, and had CFI's test *(Chief Flying Instructor)* the other day. He said "See Y landing ground?", I said yes, so he switched off the engine and said, "Do a forced landing". Orders is orders, so down I went. I had two shots which he didn't like, and when we got home I explained I hadn't been taught them. Went up with the Group Captain (Savile) yesterday as passenger, and circled the lake and studied the trenches at Ramadi.

The Political Background in Iraq

What were these 'interesting things about Iraqi politics' that Colin referred to on February 22nd? To understand what was going on at the time it is useful to trace, briefly, the history of Britain's involvement in Iraq, which stretched back to the end of World War One.

After the break-up of the Ottoman Empire Britain was given a 'Mandate' to govern Iraq for twelve years at a gathering called the Conference of San Remo in 1920. Driving this was the necessity to ensure stability while the new gold – oil – was extracted by the Anglo-Iraq Petroleum Company, which had recently set up in the country, and to build and guard the pipelines constructed to ship it back to the shores of the Mediterranean. However, the Iraqis themselves were not fooled. In an era where empires were crumbling and 'self-determination' was the buzz phrase, they saw this arrangement as 'empire by other means', and the granting of the Mandate was almost immediately followed by a violent Iraqi revolt. Within a matter of months this had cost the lives of five hundred British and Indian troops, and the British exchequer £40m, and showed no sign of abating.

It was not the only uprising in British controlled dominions that year. There was another disturbance in Somaliland, led by someone dubbed the 'Mad Mullah'. Whitehall prepared to send an expedition to quell the revolt, but were told by the Chief of the Imperial Staff that it would require two divisions. Britain was extremely hard up in 1920, exhausted and bankrupt after World War One, and, mindful of the problems in Iraq, the Government was in no mood to get involved in a costly new conflict. However, the Air Chief Marshal, Lord Trenchard, suggested that he could do the job far more cheaply with two RAF squadrons – a new arm of the armed services that had only been in existence for a few years.

Instead of large and expensive ground forces, Trenchard argued that small contingents of the RAF with the new fighters and light bombers could be used to 'fly the flag' and, as a last resort, bomb the tribes into submission. He was allowed to test his theory, and so it proved, so the strategy was immediately extended to Iraq, where the six month revolt was brought to a swift conclusion by the controversial use of phosphorous bombs. A cost effective model for controlling large areas of territory had been born.

Soon after the Iraq revolt had been quelled in this way, Britain sponsored the 'election' of King Faisal to be ruler of Iraq following a rigged plebiscite in 1921. This allowed the Foreign Office to have a 'hands off' approach, with power in the hands of a friendly ruler. And instead of garrisoning ground forces to support him, Britain gave the RAF overall control of the region. This was 'softly softly' policing 1920s style, with the threat of terror bombing from the air. Since tribesmen had rarely seen an aeroplane in those days, it is not surprising that it was so successful.

Fast forward to 1930. The Mandate was about to expire, but Britain was not quite ready to give up its influence in Iraq, because more and more oil was flowing their way. The answer was the Anglo-Iraq Treaty. In return for smoothing the path to independence, and handing over the role on internal policing, the Iraqis would permit Britain to station troops and aircraft in Iraq at two bases, with a view to helping the Iraqis in a support role to keep the tribes under control. As part of this Treaty, a new base was to be constructed sixty miles to the west of Baghdad beside Lake Habbaniya, in a bend of the River Euphrates, to house the main base and command centre of the RAF .

The new airfield complex took five years to build. When it became operational in 1935 it was 'state of the art' for comfort and efficiency. There were miles of tarmaced road bordered with oleanda and eucalyptus; luxurious married officers quarters with all the mod-cons; manicured lawns, parks and a country club; and five hundred acres of well appointed accommodation for locally enlisted staff and militia, the 'Assyrian Levies', whose job it was to guard the base. These Assyrians were Iraqis, but a minority from the north of the country, and they were thought to be more loyal that ordinary Iraqis, with a *relationship to the British Army akin to the Gurkhas – cost effective and locally based.*

There was also a polo field and a golf course, and a comfortable Imperial Airways rest house on the banks of the lake where flying boats on their way to and from India and Egypt could land, refuel and overnight. Finally, there were fields for rugby and hockey, and a sailing club.

But two crucial factors made this base different from many others the military had constructed elsewhere in the empire. Being supposedly a friendly country, where a Treaty had just been signed, and for reasons of cost, it was considered unnecessary to duplicate essential facilities like the modern water filtration plant, its water tower, and the small power station for generating electricity. So there was just one of each, making the base extremely vulnerable.

Second, the airfield itself was left outside the main perimeter fence of the camp. It was laid out on the bare desert, with no bomb-proof shelters, no dispersal areas and no defensive arrangements of any kind. It could be seen for miles around, and was overlooked from the escarpment of the Falluja Plateau.

In the late 30s life had become so quiet in Iraq that there was barely any operational flying undertaken at RAF Habbaniya at all. It became the home of the 4th Intermediate Flying Training School (IFTS), a comfortable and sleepy backwater where trainee pilots could be taught in ideal surroundings. Since 1938 the base had been under the command of a semi-retired Air Force Officer, Acting Air Chief Marshal Reginald Smart. He was a stickler for rules and routine, the perfect AOC in charge of a flying school. His team of instructors were a mix of civilian flying club instructors in uniform, with no military training, and various ex-operational RAF pilots no longer required in the front line.

This was the happy and relaxed station, far from the front line, where my father and his fellow 'Musketeers' arrived in February 1941. How ideal, and how comfortable, they were soon to find out.

169

The four ex-Indian Army officers called themselves the Four Musketeers. Pilot Officers Allan Haig, Ian Pringle, Colin, and Peter Gillespy. Only Colin and Allan Haig would survive the coming battle.

Today an hour's Audax, and some "wheeler" power approach landings. A bit of rugger, and a bit of sunbathing in the afternoons. Was out walking on the bund the other night when I met a chap who said "come in and have one". He is W/C Jope-Slade[1], in intelligence in Baghdad, and he told me a lot of interesting things about Iraqi politics.

[1] *Both Charles Braybrooks and W/C Jope-Slade were to be killed in the battle to come in May.*

March 2nd 1941

HABBANIYA

HAVE BEEN TRYING FORMATION FLYING, and am regarded as pretty dangerous at it, I think. I am also shown a forced landing, so have now got plenty to think about. The other night we went night flying. I get a bit depressed after doing three bloody awful bumps, but eventually satisfy Garner and am allowed up solo in the Audax, which is much easier. With all the lights on the camp looks like Brighton seafront at night. Life just "chills" on here, with nothing of interest to note. I flew over Ramadi with the official war map, and most of the old trenches can still be seen. (Ramadi was taken by British forces in November 1917 from the remains of the Ottoman forces).

I have got to volume III of the Official History, with one more to go after that.

March 8th 1941

HABBANIYA

HAD "LADIES NAVEL WITH CREAM" on the menu as a pudding the other day. *(A Turkish dish)*.

Did my height test, 15000 feet, successfully. Right in the clouds and could see the aerodrome occasionally. My fingertips froze and I spent the whole half hour diving and zooming, though not on purpose. I went on a cross country with Garner to Ctesiphon, Hindiya, and Falluja but I don't trust ETAs and make several blunders. We go at 6.30 am bang into the sun, and I don't see the arch until it's pointed out to me. Then solo, and I go Hit - Haditha and return in an Audax. A very pleasant trip up the Euphrates, and the villages are somewhat similar to Indian ones. Of course I tear off my navigating log and stuff it in my pocket before landing, so it won't blow away, and it blows out of my pocket whilst walking back to the flight office.

Today off in an Audax to El Aziziya, down the Tigris beyond Ctesiphon, which I find without much difficulty, though much of the ground is obscured by sandstorms. From there to Hindiya barrage and back to Falluja. The courses never work out, owing to the inaccuracies of the map, but one can usually see one's objective on the port or starboard quarter, say up to twelve miles, when the ETA is up.

Played in a sort of Cock House Match on Sunday last and won a Naafi bronze rugby medallion![1]

[1] *The Cock House Match was the final of the famous Harrow annual Football knockout competition, which some have claimed to be the precursor of the FA Cup.*

March 15th 1941

HABBANIYA

NEARLY CAUGHT OUT ON WEDNESDAY.

We were night flying, and before starting my instructor, Garner, says "be sure and use these plain flying goggles", handing me a pair – I think Christ, put them on my helmet and, when in the cockpit, I change them over for the pair with the lenses that I bought in Karachi. Then through the earphones comes:

"Are those dark bloody goggles you are wearing?'

I say yes, and I prefer them, but he makes me change them, stuffing my own pair in my pocket. So off we go, with me quivering and wondering how the hell I shall be able to see the signal light. But, actually, I can see it, and there is a full moon, so despite there being no Chance light[1]. I do four chukkas dual and then three solo in the Audax, and am fairly successful.

The CFI, Ling, gets his promotion to Wing Commander the other day and they all celebrate in style. At about 4 pm, all pickled, they make for the hangars, Levies and all, and away in the air. Luckily only one plane is crashed, landing on the polo field, but there are acrobatics near the ground, inverted circuits and God knows what. Cremin was the worst. Too pissed to convince anyone he could fly, he is taken in the back on an Audax with no parachute, and trying to bail out all the way. And coming back the same.

[1] *Mobile airfield flood lighting illuminating the landing area and the apron at night.*

March 17th 1941

I NOW OWN HALF A HORSE. Braybrooks and I were after one and asked Evans, the stable manager, if he could get one. He says "Oh yes, Finjan, £10, take over on Saturday". I arrange to ride on Thursday, but when I get there I find someone else out on him and Evans asking the fellow for £12.

I get most disgruntled, but in the meantime Braybrooks goes to the owner and offers him £10. The owner says Evans is selling it to someone else; Braybrooks thinks it's me, and says we are both in together. That gets us the horse, which Evans has in the meantime sold for £12 to the other chap. He settles it, however, by getting posted, so we get our horse, an arab chestnut and fairly tame. It's eight months since I last rode in Wana.

Yesterday met one Stoney, Armoured Cars, in the Mess, and stood him a few drinks, despite his protests, whilst his taxi was coming, and eventually he takes me off to dinner. There I meet Hilliard (also Armoured Cars) who knew Hugh, Cottingham (Gloucesters) an O.H. (Old Harrovian), and "Boozy" Bons in the R.V.R. I have a lot more whisky before dinner and shoot a line about India. Then halfway through dinner I realise suddenly that if I have another drink I can't be held responsible for the consequences. Not a comforting thought, but I preserve a calm and sober front, and manage to tell one of the bearers to get me a taxi, without anyone noticing. I stand firm against whisky, liqueurs and port and get the taxi when it arrives at 10 pm, my excuse being early flying at 5.30 am.

A messy "decontamination" when I return, and no head this morning. I go up and am unable to fly "straight and level" under the hood, performing two complete circles in fifteen minutes. Shocking!

March 25th 1941

RIDING THE HORSE AND DRINKING A LITTLE. Dan Cremin went into Baghdad the other day and cashed a cheque for five dinars in one of the local bars. He then solemnly hands them round to the nearest five chaps at the bar! Went racing last Saturday but no luck. The flying is progressing, and am still riding the waves. A letter from Ma and Peggy, and Hugh now posted as killed apparently.

Ian Pringle goes to Baghdad on Sunday and gets hold of some Greek girl there. He has come back with a scented handkerchief which he keeps under his pillow. The A/Cs on this course got some extra drill as a minor punishment and we four are made to go and look on "to see any differences etc". An old thug of a warrant officer asks us the difference between 'move to the right in threes' and 'move to the right in column' – as if we should know.

Doing loops and stall turns.

March 30th 1941

HABBANIYA

LAST NIGHT I INVITE STONEY OVER, and with Pete (Gillespy) and Charles (Braybrooks) we go to the Club.

We have some of this eggnog and some food and eventually go and play billiards. Dan Cremin appears, still drunk from the night before, and I make some passes at him with my cue. This rather takes his fancy and the next hour I spend chasing him and others and doing points and withdrawals at all and sundry in a welter of flung water and pullings away of carpets from under one's feet. All in the form of raids from the billiard room. We get quite pally and then I go home in a taxi, reckoning I have had enough.

I find I've left my key in the Club so walk back for it. I stay for some more booze and get confidential with Dan C. For some reason or other 'socking' is mentioned and I stick out my jaw to him and invite one. I get it too, a right-hand swing, which staggers me and is about all I can take. I am sober enough to refrain from hitting him back, and Garner comes in to make the peace. Back at last at 2.00 am with Broughton, sentimentally drunk despite his bare 21 years.

Today I go out on Finjan to Medling Defile and back along the bund amongst gardens and date palms. Met Geary from Shaibah in the Club last night and one Hibbens of 3⁄4 Rajputs who's in Intelligence here.

Johnson and K.S. Smith, my drinking companions from Kenya, have gone – to the Middle East and Shaibah respectively. I have completed the small book on Arabic, though the words therein are committed to a very faulty memory, but have stuck at "Measures of the Verb", the Mesopotamian grammar. The interpreter who professes to instruct me says I am capable of passing the colloquial exam; which was worth ID15 (extra pay) before the war; but I don't believe him.

The Greeks all got drunk (not unusual) the other night when the news came that Yugoslavia had turned out their pro-German party. The result of this was some very excellent singing though I was endeavouring to sleep at the time and so didn't appreciate it. But I could just picture them with a bottle and/or girl in each hand.

April 4th 1941

HABBANIYA

COMPLETED MY 10 HOURS BLIND FLYING, and worn out a few instructors in the process I think. I have an hour to go to complete sixty-five hours of Intermediate Training, and next week we have our exams in ground work. Shades of Sandhurst again. Finjan turning out to be a polo pony, I have a couple of turns on him at the game, but am not very good at it; rather like my hockey, the ball goes under the bat too often. I go shooting with my Winchester

175

for jackal, who live out on the plateau, but they see me first and disappear into small holes (caves almost).

Letter from Ma and Peggy and Hugh posted as killed. All my damned fault for tempting fortune by what I said to Bill in a letter. Uncle Bill said he "saw" he would get through all right, so trusting to Tiree second sight I never even bothered to scan the casualty reports.

Was shown slow rolls, rolls off the top and flick rolls, but have had no solo in which to practice them.

The incessant cooing of turtle doves here recalls Assam all the time, and there is also a variety of paddy birds, locally called storks, which is exactly the noise they make, like death rattling his dice. Then there's the sergeant/pilot bird which, at dawn and dusk, goes cookadoo, cookadoo-la.

Ian had a letter from Fairweather in Karachi and they are not coming here after all. The AOC happened to inspect Karachi Aero Club and happened to catch Jhadu or someone lecturing on ground subjects. So Bill Jones got his head chewed off and no wonder!! Mess bills about ID 10 *(Iraqi dinars)*.

INSTRUCTORS, "B" FLIGHT 4 IFTS

C.F.I. W/C "Larry" Ling
(gentleman but talks like Aunt Vivien)
F/Lt D.A. Cremin "Dan"
(never sober)
F/O D.A. Garner "Stooge"
(ex-policeman)
F/O H. Broadhurst
(ex-club instructor)
F/O J. Broughton
(21 and a gentleman)
Sgt "Joey" Baker
(definitely no gentleman)

April 8th 1941

ALARMS AND EXCURSIONS.

A few days ago the Regent was smuggled out of the country, the Prime Minister resigned, and the Army took over, one of the generals endeavouring to form a cabinet. Then occurs the most colossal flap. He is supposed to be anti-British, so the planes are bombed up, arms and ammunition dished out, everyone made to wear uniform and walk about armed, and no one allowed outside the camp. Yesterday an Iraqi aeroplane arrived, did three circuits and landed. The Gladiators were unable to get up to shoot him down, as they had been ordered to ring up the AOC before they took off, and his telephone was engaged. Chaps rush out to arrest the pilot, who says he has merely come for a meteorological exam, and he's right too.

Today a colossal formation is organised over Falluja and Ramadi, but there is so much low-lying cloud that it is postponed. The German news says we are prisoners of war and that Italian transports have arrived in Basra to take us away! And that the Iraqis have shot down some eighteen British planes![1]

[1] *A very interesting comment. According to the official history, the British were blissfully unaware at this stage that any real threat from the Iraqis existed, and that Rachid Ali's sudden attack three weeks later was entirely unexpected, but here is evidence that it was already being talked about, if only via German propaganda.*

April 11th 1941

HABBANIYA

IAN (PRINGLE) AND I PUT IN FOR WEEKEND LEAVE on the routine Valencia to Tel Aviv, and should have gone today if it hadn't been for the damn trouble.

The Situation in Iraq in April 1941

After the signing of the Ango-Iraq Treaty in 1930, although life had seemed deceptively quiet at Habbaniya, tensions had been rising across the country. There had always been a certain amount of inter-ethnic rivalry between Sunnis and Shias, as well as with the minority Christian Assyrian population, but in 1933 it had taken a turn for the worse, when the Iraqi army, under the prime minister-ship of Rachid Ali, had massacred 3000 Assyrian women and children at Simele, in an attempt to ethnically cleanse the northern provinces. This caused much anger amongst the Assyrian Levies, especially when their British masters refused to allow them home to help. Soon after the massacre the pro-British King Faisal died, leaving a much weaker heir, King Ghazi, on the throne. Rachid Ali resigned. However, the Germans saw an opportunity to weaken Britain's position, and they dispatched a T.E. Lawrence type character called Fritz Grobba to present his credentials to the the young and impressionable new King. Grobba's strategy was to gain influence with the Arab nationalists, and foment their growing opposition against the British and the French across the Middle East. Initially it was all about trade, but increasingly, Iraqi army officers began to be invited for training in Germany.

As the 30s wore on, the weak and ineffectual King Ghazi faced mounting tribal tensions until, in 1938, a group of Iraqi army officers known as the Golden Square seized power, bringing Rachid Ali back as prime minister. Groomed by Grobba, they were virulently anti-British, and they refused to declare war on Germany in 1939 as required under their treaty obligations, though Grobba was sent home. Suddenly Britain's toehold in Iraq began to look less secure.

So by 1940, despite the death of Ghazi in 1939 in a car accident (which many blamed on the British) and his replacement by a child king and pro-British Regent, relations with the military backed government were tense, with the British embassy in Baghdad reporting increasing activity between the Iraqis and the Axis powers.

To add further to British concerns, the Iraqi government allowed the Italian legation to remain open in Baghdad after Italy came into the war in June 1940, and secret plans were drawn up to divert Iraq's oil pipeline to Syria.

In early 1941, just a few days after Colin arrived, events took a further twist - Rachid Ali was ousted by a pro-British prime minister, Al Hashimi. During February and March the British worked on plans with Al Hashimi to remove the colonels of the Golden Square from their posts, but before they could act, a second coup took place on April 1st, and Rachid Ali was brought back. The original plot was to assassinate the Regent, but he managed to escape to the American Embassy dressed as a woman, before being driven down to Habbaniya in the boot of the American ambassador's car, from where he was flown out to Jordan on the 3rd April.

The British were now in a most vulnerable position. All military traffic between Baghdad and Habbaniya was stopped by the new Iraqi government, and the ambassador's radio equipment was confiscated, the embassy going into lockdown (Freya Stark was holed up there during this period). On 6th April Air Vice Marshal Smart cabled General Wavell in Cairo and the Air Ministry in London asking for reinforcements. However, his request came at a bad time - Rommel was advancing at lightning speed across North Africa and the British were on the retreat from Crete. April 1941 was probably the darkest month in the entire war from a British perspective. Wavell refused the request, recommending a diplomatic solution. Habbaniya were on their own.

So Smart organised that time honoured form of sabre-rattling, the 'demonstration flight', as recorded by Colin on April 11th. Another participant, Squadron Leader Tony Dudgeon, remembers it in his book 'Hidden Victory':

"48 pilots we managed to find, and so 48 aircraft flew. All instructors flew of course, plus a few of the more advanced pupils, and a couple of Greek pilots. Several different types were chosen – 32 Harts and Audaxes, 13 twin engined Oxfords and the three Gladiator biplane-fighters. Those out of date fighters, of course, were not flown by fighter pilots. They were only based (at Habbaniya) because they had been superannuated from the Western Desert theatre as being beyond practical use in a fighting role. They were kept as a sort of flying sports-car for Headquarters officers to use for any local travelling. This great gaggle – it deserved no better word – took to the air. As may be imagined from the comparatively unpractised rag, tag and bobtail in the pilot's seats, the quality of the formation itself was terrible. There were five flights in all. One each of Oxfords and Harts, and two of Audaxes, all cruising at the same speed and, God willing, in the same direction. The three fighters, flying faster, had a roving commission and swooped around, above and below the main formation. Fortunately, no aircraft came into collision. The whole of this lot traipsed back and forth near two local villages called Ramadi and Falluja."

'The Demonstration flight'. The formation flight of April 10th over Falluja and Ramadi.

We do a formation flight the other day of four squadrons – Harts with Oxfords circling overhead, and the three Gladiators down below. I went in Dan Cremin's front seat and we went over Falluja and Ramadi. Ling showed me the air photographs of Falluja showing an anti-aircraft gun there. Heard last night that thirty Indian Battalions arrived the other day in Basra, being "Niblick" force. Alan Haig very drunk in the Club on neat whisky.

The 'Thirty Indian battalions' have now turned into a few Iraqi army troops.

April 14th 1941

HABBANIYA

THE 'ANTI-AIRCRAFT GUN' IS IDENTIFIED as a field kitchen.

Dined with young Stoney the other night and sampled some Mount Carmel wine. We discuss women – or rather they do. Letter

181

from old Mike, in 2/West Yorks, with 2FFR and 6/13 GR down in the Sudan I believe. Today they decided to discontinue training and form two operational squadrons, ITS becoming Audaxes and ATS *(Advanced training school)* an Oxford squadron. I get detailed to the Oxfords as a bomb aimer of all things. When the hell will we get away – I hate to think.

Was graded an 'average' pilot, which isn't so bad as I fully expected "below average".

April 17th 1941

HABBANIYA

GOT MY 'WINGS' YESTERDAY. Went up and found W/V *(wind velocity)* by the three-course method in an Oxford and didn't do too badly.

Then a big flap yesterday and another formation flight ordered, this time presumably over Baghdad. I get a Hart to myself in S/Ldr Platsis's flight and we "stand to" from 8-11.30 when it is cancelled. Aircraft dispersed everywhere, and all over the polo ground too.

Piles of leaflets, printed in Jerusalem and Cairo, have arrived, so I hope I am allowed to drop some. Pete didn't get his 'wings', having failed in navigation. A year ago I had the mustard gas, and the mark is still on my forearm.

April 21st 1941

HABBANIYA

CAMERA OBSCURA AND WIND FINDING in Oxfords. Then the other night Ling says something about "Dunford Wood my ace operational pilot". I say "eh?" and then discover he didn't know I was in the Oxfords.

So today I go back to B flight and do message picking up, with White as my first passenger. My flying is shocking since it's a month since I last flew solo, and I can hardly see the message poles. I miss first time and second time break a pole; then it's time for breakfast. Irwin, Wall, Fairweather and Humphries (who went and married Mary Simpson in Karachi) arrive. They wear uniform all day in India now apparently.

Troops arrive from India at Basra. The King's Own came in Atlantas, B.T.s (with Dudley Withers) and Douglases. Also 2/8 GR with Mick Mackenzie and now, some say, 1/13 from Quetta.

April 27th 1941

HABBANIYA

I READ IN "AEROPLANE" about a new Waziristan medal for operations from December 16th 1937 to December 31st 1939, so Teddie Humphries, Reggie Wall and myself go out and buy one and post it up. After all these years, too. Douglases keep ferrying troops up here, and most of the King's Own are here. I met Nigel Gribbon and Byers in the Club last night. A most enjoyable party, majority army, from which I escaped at about midnight. Fairweather, Boozy Bons and myself get together over our black rifle buttons and get very confidential about it. The great thing to do is to exchange buttons. "Tiny" Irwin now has his own, free Greek, free French, RAF, RIASC and 16th Punjab, all on his tunic.

A.T.S. starts tomorrow, and I and Haig are in Stonehill's flight. 1/13 GR are not in Basra after all – it's the 2nd or 3rd battalion, 11th Sikhs.

I go to the Lake Hotel today with Wall and all the Malayan pupils. Also with us is Richardson, ex-navy and Imperial airways pilot, commissioned as a pilot officer for a fortnight to fly the Douglases from India, where he was holding a ground job in I.N.A. (India National Airways). Drinks and lunch and the conversation hops from Malaya to Bombay and down to Kenya, with interludes in Canada, and then back again to Singapore every time.

*'BOAC on Lake Habbaniya'. A BOAC Short Empire flying boat (G-AETX)
taking on passengers. The last flying boat flew out on
April 30th.*

Polo today but Finjan is a bit slow and wants some spurs. A pity that one can't have a few drinks and enjoy a party without having to have too many and stay up half the night. I reckon my system is the best, of parking drinks I don't want about the place, and if that is no good, of making myself sick when I come back of an evening.

April 30th 1941

Habbaniya

YESTERDAY EVENING ALL BRITISH WOMEN and children were evacuated from Baghdad, and it is said that the Iraqis were about to resist a landing of further troops to add to the force already here. This morning the alarm goes at about 4.00 am and we go down to the flights and prepare planes for war. An Iraqi officer comes in by car to the AOC *(Air Vice Marshal Smart)* and out again, presumably with some sort of ultimatum. Then troops and armoured cars appear on the plateau, and at 8.00 am I go off with James Fairweather to reconnoitre them. I keep her at 1000 feet and we see three guns, nine or so AFVs and about one battalion of troops all lined up ready to fire at the camp. I then land her on the polo pitch and we report to AHQ. A shave and wash and some breakfast, and now what!?

Just done a two hour recce of the Plateau, Falluja and Falluja Plain in an Audax with Sgt Douglas, 13.30 to 15.30. What a time! Saw eighteen horse drawn 18-pounders the other side of Falluja Plain, and Bofors guns, howitzers and M/Gs on the Plateau. Simply grand at 500 feet and AOC very pleased with my report, and asks me to do a dawn patrol. I tell Ling and he says "Yes! Yes!" and details Haig for it according to his roster. Very tired, and with one of those chronic thirsts for iced water which I sometimes get.

May 1st 1941

HABBANIYA

FLAP! FLAP!

Pete does a forced landing on Falluja Plain near the cement factory on his recce. I go up afterwards and much as usual, only they seem to have less troops on the plateau. I count twelve horse-drawn guns, but Allan makes it twenty-five. Ling gives us some maps made in 1918 and they're good, but roads etc have to be put in. We now have to stick to 2000 feet so will not be able to see anything. No more steep turns at 250 feet!

2130: C/O has told us we attack Iraqis at 0500 tomorrow. Under Ian as C/O our flight is ordered to stand by from 0500.

May 3rd 1941

WAR!

I went up at sunrise in the back of Broadhurst's Audax, without a parachute like a fool, and we drop 20lb bombs on the guns in conjunction with Oxfords and Wellingtons from Shaibah. I use the rear gun on an escaping lorry, but it's so damn hard when pulling out of a dive.

Next sortie I go up with Broughton, but we go too low and I feel something tug at my sleeve. Then liquid comes back over me, which to my horror I find to be blood. I can't see out of my goggles so stand up and find Jimmy B. in front is shot through the face and blood pouring out like a perforated petrol tank. I buckle on my parachute, but luckily he is fully conscious and we land on the polo pitch OK. I am a bit shaken, and we then get shelled on the polo ground and in the mess, without much effect. Ling, Garner and Broughton get shot, and Chico Walsh with two pupils Skelton and Robinson is shot down in flames in an Oxford.

Dan Cremin orders us four to do a continual patrol to Baghdad with R/T. I do one at about 11 am, and over Falluja Plain meet three Gladiators, but they pass me by and I take it they are ours. I see thirteen troop lorries on the plain and do a little front gunning, though not very successfully. We get shot up and bombed in the camp by Bredas, Savoia Marchettis, Northrops and "Peggy" Audaxes, but no damage round me.

These Iraqis have guts I must say. We are a bit windy about these Bredas, as we think of ours as a "suicide patrol" – we are sitting meat for them, we haven't been taught the slightest thing about air combat.

Pete (Gillespy) goes off at 3.00 pm and at 4.00 we get worried as he hasn't been heard of for an hour. At 4.30 Ian (Pringle) goes off on the patrol and finds his burnt-out plane in the desert near Falluja. He is himself attacked by a Breda with tracer but escapes. I

'C squadron (Audaxes) on the Polo ground'.
Alongside are the operations tents.

do a patrol to Najaf in the evening, windy as hell. I see a Gladiator and am off "through the gate" without waiting to see whose it was.

This morning at dawn there's a heavy shelling of the polo ground and, it seems, the room next to mine. Today I do a photography job, or try to (knowing nothing about it), over the Plateau and up to "Palm Grove". I keep at 6000 feet as their A/A stuff is known to fall down again at 5000 feet. Later we all do a bit of dive bombing. I am told how to let go the quadrant and a rough idea of it, and off I go. I thought I pulled out between 1500 and 2000 feet but anyway, my plane is U/S on return, and several bullets have just missed the water jacket. Funnily enough, after the pullout, I went sharp left, but all my holes were on the starboard side! All this is by Dhibban Village and do we give them hell! Dan Cremin and his boys! Phew!

Not much shelling after this morning's effort, and the Savoias don't do much damage. Dicky Cleaver in a Gladiator is seen to make a steep dive with smoke pouring out of it. We are lucky operating from the polo ground, and the operations tent is a sight to see. The

RAF Habbaniya Air Striking Force

Commanding Officer
Group Captain W.A.B. Saville

A Squadron
Wing Commander Selyn-Roberts
10 Hawker Audax (8 x 20lb bombs)

B Squadron
Squadron Leader Dudgeon
26 Airspeed Oxfords (8 x 20lb bombs)
(Previously the ATS's main training aircraft)
7 Fairey Gordons (2 x 250lb bombs)
(Previously used for target towing)
1 Blenheim Mk1

C Squadron
Wing Commander Ling
10 Hawker Audax (2 x 250lb bombs)

D Squadron
Wing Commander Hawtrey
12 Hawker Audax (2 x 250lb bombs)

Gladiator Fighter Flight
Flight Lt Cleaver
9 Gladiator fighters

Communications Flight
Flight Lt Skeet
2 Valentia (4 x 500lb bombs)
1 Valentia (8 x 250lb bombs)

The Battle Develops

In the weeks of rising tension that followed the coup in Baghdad, a number of instructors of the flying school had taken the initiative - without official sanction according to later reports - to ready their motley collection of superannuated biplanes for action. A key impetus had been the arrival in early April of Squadron Leader Dudgeon, who had been sent for some 'time out' and 'R+R' after completing fifty missions in the Western Desert, suffering from exhaustion. However, with his combat experience, he was ideally suited to team up with Wing Commander Ling in his unofficial project to convert their ancient Audaxes into bombers, designing bomb brackets and cobbling together ammunition. Both officers could see how the situation was developing, and that if they did nothing, their fledgling pupil pilots in their lightly armed trainers would be sitting ducks. Though Colin does not mention it in his diaries, one source of knowledge tapped by Dudgeon and Ling were the 'four musketeers', as these ex-Indian army officers, especially Colin, had first hand knowledge of how Hawker Audax biplanes had been used to bomb tribesmen on the North West Frontier.

They also recognised that the airfield they operated from was extremely vulnerable, being outside the perimeter of the camp and overlooked by the Plateau. After some quite considerable lobbying of the camp commandant, they managed to get hold of some bulldozers to flatten the polo ground and make it ready to take aircraft, beyond line of sight of the escarpment. It was from the polo ground that two of the reformed squadrons operated during the battle, and where many of the pilots slept in tents, yards from their planes.

Despite the refusal of aid from Wavell in early April, Smart was offered help from Auchinleck in India, who proposed diverting the 10th Indian Division (embarked at Karachi and ready to go to Malaya) to Basra. It turned out to be a lucky escape. The first elements, a brigade strong, sailed on 12th April, landing on the 18th, while four hundred troops of the Kings Own Royal Regiment flew direct to Habbaniya in transport planes in the world's first strategic airlift. As required under treaty, the British ambassador, Cornwallis, was obliged to notify the Iraqi Government of these troop movements, which he did at the last moment. Rachid Ali had no right to refuse permission, but he demanded they transit the country as quickly as possible, and it spurred him to accelerate his demands for help of his own from the Axis powers. When Cornwallis informed him on 23rd April that a second brigade would be landing, Ali flatly refused to allow it, declaring it an act of war. The disembarkation went ahead. It was then that Rachid Ali decided he had to make his move, as intercepted messages with the Germans revealed. He decided to march on Habbaniya.

It was at this point that Cornwallis, sensing a showdown was coming, asked Rachid Ali for permission to evacuate British women and children from Baghdad to Habbaniya. Their arrival is recorded by Colin in his diary entry of the 30th, and they reported sharing the road with advancing Iraqi troops, which Colin reconnoitred from the air the same day.

Faced with the Iraqi ultimatum to surrender, and reluctant to start a war without higher authority, Smart cabled London for orders. Eventually they came, direct from Churchill: 'Strike hard. Use all available force'.

In addition to the troops landing at Basra, Wellington bombers were sent from Egypt, and these 'Wimpeys' as referenced by Colin, took part in the initial strike. But the quickest route for relief to arrive was across 500 miles of desert from Egypt, so as soon as word of the outbreak of hostilities reached the Air Ministry, the Prime Minister and Chiefs of Staff cabled Wavell to put a relief force together. Wavell was again reluctant - first, he maintained it was India Command's responsibility to relieve Habbaniya and second, he had his hands full and feared a region-wide Arab revolt if a full scale war developed with Rachid Ali. He urged a diplomatic settlement. However, he was overruled by Churchill on 3rd May, and ordered to organise help. Reluctantly, Wavell acquiesced. Called Habforce, it was made *up of mostly under-equipped and poorly trained peacekeeping forces from Palestine (all that Wavell could spare), many of whom were trained as cavalry but no longer had horses. In fact their lack of a means of transport was so severe that city buses and trucks had to be commandeered from the streets of Jerusalem to transport them across the desert. They were ready to march on 11th May. A rapid advance column called Kingcol, with members of the Arab legion under Pasha Glubb, spearheaded the force, racing ahead in the best available transport to capture the wells at Rutbah en route. Without those, Habforce would not have enough water to get to Habbaniya. They finally arrived on 17th May - some days after the siege had been broken by the pilots of 4 IFTS, as Colin recounts over the following days. This march across the desert, chronicled by Somerset de Chair in 'The Golden Carpet', has the air of a 'Boys Own' adventure, and was described by Glubb as "one of the most remarkable examples of military daring in history."*

C.O. came up and said would we remove the empty bottles. None of my work, as I wait until we finish at dusk for mine.

Yesterday the Iraqis apparently listened in on their R/T and as soon as they heard the fighter patrols going home, in they came. But today the "Wimpys" *(Vickers Wellington Bombers, flying from Basra)* blow up Hinaidi *(Iraqi Air Force base outside Baghdad)* and nothing comes over after that.

Poor old Pete! I hope he was able to jump out. Water restrictions reduced, and we can now use the showers. The baths are kept filled with spare drinking water, but of course the Greeks have to go and jump in with their soap – if they use any.

May 4th 1941

HABBANIYA

SHELLING LAST NIGHT FROM 9.30 – 12.30 and then again at 4 am. I lie quaking in my bed, but they don't seem to do much damage. This morning we are all split into four-hour "watches" so I get a bit of time off in my bed and get a good shower. I go up in the back of Dan's plane on a bund bombing job, but 20-pounders are too small for the job. Then I fly a plane off the aerodrome onto the polo ground, and land dead across wind, with no ill effects.

A mechanised column took Rutbah and reached "H4" landing ground on the pipeline yesterday. Hope they get here before the Germans do.[1]

Blenheims and "Wimpeys" attack Hinaidi again today. Had a drink with Nigel Gribbon. Wish I had Attam Khan here (his bearer in Waziristan), as all the bearers are hiding under their beds in the civil cantonment and nothing is done. A plane is up continuously tonight so hope there will be no more shelling and I will get some sleep. Charles Braybrooks killed in a Vincent down Shaibah way. So poor old Sheila Nicholson in 'Pindi will be weeping. A few shells this evening before Dan Cremin took off.

I hear my photography job was pretty useless!

[1] *The relief column – Habforce – had not yet even been assembled in Egypt and Palestine, and would not leave until 11th, so this rumour is false. Evidently British propaganda was meant as much for spine-stiffening their own beleaguered garrison at Habbaniya as frightening the Iraqis. Second, it is interesting to note that the Germans are already being talked about as 'on their way'. Likewise, they were not to arrive for at least a week, and in fact their help had only been requested by the Iraqis some days previously.*

May 5th 1941

HABBANIYA

MORE SHELLING AT DAWN and at 9.00 am today, despite patrols in the air all night. Pat Weir and a platoon of King's Own do a successful raid Dhibban way last night, without any casualties. I am on at dawn, 4.15, then off 5-9, on 9-1, off 1-5 and on again to dusk. Mostly sitting around in our operations tent while "Doug" Baker presides with three telephones, fixes everything up, serves beer and washes up the glasses, besides having the tent cleaned out. With the help of W.O. Shawn Sheagh, R.E., we snaffle some ice to keep the beer cold in a zinc-lined parachute box which is the frigidaire.

I go up before lunch to bomb four cars in a copse and undershoot them. Then at dusk Dan, Gordon Arthur, Alan and myself go up to spot the guns at their dusk shelling. I am just coming home as the sun has disappeared when I see other planes in the air, so reckon I had better stay up a bit longer. I turn and notice a flash in a copse. I climb up and drop four bombs on the wrong copse, then four bombs on the right one (near "Camel Turn"), all of which overshoot. But I get in three good long bursts with my front gun at it, and Cpl Sanderson in the back does some good work with his Lewis gun. I report to P/O Shotter in the ops rooms, find the copse on a photographic map, and they are all pleased as it is a new one. I then find there was no shelling at the time I saw the flash, so it can't have been a gun!

'Iraqi M.T. at Canal Turn'. The remains of the Iraqi convoy.

May 6th 1941

HABBANIYA

I GO UP AT DAWN TO LOOK FOR MY GUN, with James Fairweather in the back, and find it's not there. How I take off I don't know, as it's almost pitch dark. Sit about doing nothing until 3.30 pm. The Kings Own attack and are held up at "Hell Fire Corner", the ridge above Dhibban. Dan Cremin and his boys (minus me) go and shoot it up, and they all come back riddled with holes. I get up eventually with "Tiny" Irwin in the back and machine gun the fleeing troops. They stop and shoot me up, but it seems slaughter all the same. Three Iraqi armoured cars come up, my bombs miss but Dan opens them up like a tin opener with a stick right down the road. Tony warns me they "bite" so I don't go too low.

Northrops come over while I am eating lunch in the tent at 3.30 and drop bombs right across the polo ground and get one of our "recco" Audaxes. The fire spreads to a Gladiator. Dicky Cleaver and Bob May wounded and some killed. Last night at

12.30 some 20lbers are dropped by Iraqi Audaxes and come very near my room. They also riddle our tent with bullet holes. Then a convoy approaches from Falluja and the boys go off, including Ian (Pringle), it being his turn. As he is buckling on his parachute I say to myself "He won't come back", and sure enough he doesn't. He does several trips and then Alan (Haig) and I go up. Both sections of the convoy are in flames, between "Canal Turn" and Falluja, and I put some bombs on the road and a good burst with my front gun. Two trips I do, and on the second I bend one bombing quadrant and am unable to even use the other, it being so stiff. So I use the front gun and return home, during another raid at about 6.00 pm. Some funny holes on the polo ground, like aerial torpedos, and they were obviously aiming for our line of tents. They must reckon 3 squadron the most dangerous one! Well, Stonhill sees a plane dive into the ground near the convoy at about 6.15, and it turns out to be Ian with Fairbrother in the back. But his bombs blew up, so he wouldn't have known much! What's the use? Hooray for the next man to die – Alan Haig or me.[1]

[1] Of the four pupil pilot officers from the Indian Army – the 'Four Musketeers' – who had met at the medical in Delhi in October and who had started the course at Habbaniya together, two – Ian Pringle and Pete Gillespy – were now dead.

May 8th 1941

HABBANIYA

I DON'T GO FLYING YESTERDAY. A bit of tip-and-run bombing from "Peggy" Audaxes, one of which is shot down by a Blenheim fighter. A Savoia and a Northrop spotted force landed in the desert, and are destroyed after a prodigious amount of bombs, S.A.A. (small arms ammunition) and Very lights have been used on them. Dan Cremin returning from the furthermost one meets a "Peggy" Audax going home, but as his front gun had jammed he does nothing. But the two planes on the ground are at 65 degrees

Fliegerfuehrer Irak

Just as the British were sending help from other theatres of war, so the Rachid Ali government was desperately seeking military aid from the Axis powers. And not just arms and money, but planes and personnel. Because he had been forced to act before he was ready, on account of the 10th Indian division's landing at Basra, the support he had been asking for since coming back to power in early April had not yet been signed off in Berlin, so in the days after his attack on the camp, a scramble was on to organise a taskforce. Not only the British were stretched - the Germans were too, with preparations for Operation Barbarossa well advanced and the invasion of Crete about to kick off. But Grobba (since 1939 in Berlin) persuaded Von Ribbontrop, and through him Hitler, that here was a golden opportunity to drive a wedge between Egypt and Britain's dominions in the east, and moreover to deprive Egypt and India of the oil that flowed from Iraq. There was also the tantalising prospect of diverting it to support Barbarossa instead.

So on 6th May Colonel Werner Junck of the Luftwaffe was tasked with taking a squadron of ME110 fighter bombers and a squadron of Heinkel 111 bombers via Syria to Mosul - the 'Fliegerfuehrer Irak' - which were diverted from Greece. Swift negotiations were concluded with Vichy France (the 'Paris Protocols'), allowing Italian and German forces to transit Syria, captured British arms to be released from there to the Iraqis, and a Luftwaffe base to be established in Aleppo. On 11th May Grobba returned to Baghdad to coordinate aid, and the first elements of the Luftwaffe arrived over the next couple of days, along with a Major Axel Von Blomberg, who was to act as liaison between the Axis and Iraqi air forces. Unfortunately he was killed by a freak bullet as his plane came in to land at Baghdad, fired by an Iraqi sentry who mistook the plane for the RAF.

However, the Luftwaffe was quickly in action, making an immediate impression by attacking Kingcol at Rutbah and Habbaniya on 15th - as recorded in Colin's diary. However, the next

YEAR 1941 MONTH DATE	AIRCRAFT Type	No.	PILOT OR 1ST PILOT	2ND PILOT, PUPIL OR PASSENGER	DUTY (INCLUDING RESULTS AND REMARKS)
					TOTALS BROUGHT FORWARD
April 21st	Audax	7514	Self	Lac White	Message Picking Up
" 22nd	Hart T"	4416	Sgt Baker	Self	Front Gun Dual
" 23rd	Audax	K7514	Self	Solo	Forced Landings
" 24th	Hart	K4021	Self	Solo	Polo ground to Aerodrome
" 28th	HART T	4916	Sgt Horsham	SELF	I.F. SPINS IRAQ ARMY POSITIONS
" 30th	"	4896	SELF	LT FAIRWEATHER	RECCO. OF PLATEAU IRAQ ARMY DISPOSITIONS
" "	AUDAX	7530	SELF	SGT DOUGLAS	RECCO. PLATEAU — FALLUJA PLAIN IRAQ ARMY DISPOSITIONS
MAY 1ST	AUDAX	7518	SELF	SGT DOUGLAS	——— Do ——— Do IRAQ REBELLION
" 2ND	AUDAX	7543	SELF	SGT DOUGLAS	OPERATIONS ——— Do
" "	"	7518	"	"	RECCE MATARA CANAL
" 3RD	AUDAX	7530	SELF	CPL COPEROD	OPERATIONS — PHOTOGRAPHY (PLANE US) SOMS EL BAHRAN
" "	"	5107	"	SOLO	OPERATIONS — DIVE BOMBING — FRONT GUN
MAY 4th	AUDAX	5105	SELF	SOLO	AERODROME — POLO GROUND
MAY 5TH	AUDAX	7504	SELF	LT IRWIN	OPERATIONS — SIRRIYA BOND
" "	"	3714	SELF	SOLO	AERODROME — POLO GROUND
" "	AUDAX	7514	SELF	CPL SANDERSON	OPERATIONS — GUN IN COPSE
" 6TH	AUDAX	7503	SELF	P/O FAIRWEATHER	OPERATIONS — RECCE. GUN IN COARSE
" "	"	3107	SELF	SOLO	AERODROME — POLO GROUND
" "	"	3099	SELF	SOLO	OPERATIONS — CONVOY FALLUJA ROAD
" "	"	3099	SELF	SOLO	OPERATIONS — CONVOY FALLUJA ROAD
" 8TH	AUDAX	7521	SELF	SOLO	OPERATIONS — DAWN PATROL
" "	"	7503	SELF	P/O IRWIN	OPERATIONS — PATROL FALLUJA - PLATEAU
" "	"	7525	SELF	LAC WILLIAMS	OPERATIONS — PATROL FALLUJA - MATARA
MAY 9TH	AUDAX	7530	SELF	SGT HAYLES	OPERATIONS — CONTACT PATROL MATARA ?
			GRAND TOTAL [Cols. (1) to (10)] 149 Hrs. 10 Mins.		TOTALS CARRIED FORWARD

Colin's pilot's flying log book entries covering the beginning of the battle. Not all sorties are entered here - in particular the first sort he made in the back of Broughton's Audax at dawn on the 5th.

day three Hurricanes arrived from Egypt to reinforce Habbaniya, as well as several more Gladiators and Blenheims, which took the fight to the Germans, attacking the Luftwaffe planes on the ground at Rachid air base on the 17th and again on the 18th.

After just two days, the Luftwaffe lost 30% of their strength. Although some Italian fighters started arriving in late May, by then the Germans were almost spent, and the Iraqi air force had been destroyed. It was too little, too late.

so when this is plotted on the map it leads to Baquba. Yesterday afternoon they bomb it, Stonhill, Broadhurst, Haig and Frewin, and only three come back. I am convinced it's Alan, but no, Stonhill was seen to force land near Baquba, so he must be a prisoner.

The C.O. wants to change our name to 4 Fighting Training School, which sounds OK. Night flying last night and they make me standby pilot, so I sleep out by our tent in a ditch on a camp bed. Today I do a recco of the Plateau and go down to fifty feet, and there's nothing to be seen between the camp and Palm Grove – Majara Road. I look at the convoy and see all the corpses. There is a platoon of Levies above Dhibban, and a section of our armoured cars above on the Plateau, manoeuvring and stalking Dan's burnt-out armoured cars at Canal Turn.

May 9th 1941

Habbaniya

I DO TWO MORE RECCO PATROLS YESTERDAY and front gun a gun team (horses) on Falluja plain. Most of the time is spent low flying over the area and taking photographs with my camera. A sergeant pilot in an Oxford, at 2000 feet over Ramadi, has one shot fired at him and it goes through his heart. I go down to view all the booty in A.S.U. (ammunition storage unit) and get myself an 18lb shell case. There are all the guns and armoured cars and a wicked little Italian "whippet" tank. Some Valencias came up from Shaibah the other day and lost the way. One had to land at Hit, where the crew and passengers (15 Kings Own) surrendered after burning the plane. Galiani (Rachid Ali) has fled to Turkey, according to the BBC, after riots in Baghdad, so I suppose this little war is now over. The Blenheims raid Mosul yesterday, and one gets shot up and they have to bail out up there. Five hours flying yesterday and damned tired, with "parachute bottom". I get myself issued with an Iraqi .38 at the depot by saying I haven't got a gun, so it can't really be classified as "loot" or "booty".

198

Entry from the daily bulletin of 8th May, with the message to AVM Smart from Churchill.

May 10th 1941

HABBANIYA

I DO A SORT OF CONTACT PATROL as our forces occupy Najara, going out with them as a guardian angel. Very hazy today, and I sit about in the tent all day, gradually getting deeper and deeper in dust. As soon as my goggles break, I suppose I shall have to confess to my sins, as I can't fit my spare pair of lenses. They need the edges filing down a little first.[1]

Gruesome stories around of what the Levies did to any prisoners they captured the other day. Most of them are Assyrians, and have a lot to pay back. Pat Weir has been put in for an M.C. – his platoon came under severe M/G fire, and he silenced one lot with a V.B. fired from the shoulder. He then waved his platoon on and got a bullet in the uplifted arm, severing a main artery. Some Madras sappers and miners arrive by Douglas *(DC3 aircraft)* today.

[1] *Due to his poor eyesight, Colin relied on his specially made pair of google with lenses that he had specially made in India.*

199

May 12th 1941

115 DEGREES YESTERDAY, and boy was it hot in our tent. I go out on a bombing raid to Musaib, where there is an arms factory, but fail to hit anything. Then this morning a two-hour patrol from 4.15 with Tiny (Irwin) to Falluja, El Musaib, Najara and round the back of the Lake to Ramadi. There I attempt to drop a stick of bombs on some barges, but am bloody useless at dive bombing.

Alan and I do Pete and Ian's things the other day, packing them up etc, and a more depressing job I never had. (Gillespy and Pringle, killed in the first days of the battle). We sort of give them each a dressing gown (no idea who's is who's) and share out the shoes evenly. I collect all Pete's bills and give them to the adjutant who will have some fun sorting them out.

Rashid Ali is still in Baghdad (not fled to Turkey as reported on the BBC), and a Heinkel was seen today at Hinaidi whilst they were bombing it. I should think my time will soon be up, unless I can keep up this deception. However, Quien Sabe! I forget all my Arabic by now. Nigel Gribbon in hospital with a nice bullet in his leg.

May 13th 1941

HABBANIYA

A FEW HEINKELS REPORTED by the British minister at Beirut, and the Turkish consul at Mosul. Russia has recognised Rachid Ali, so what to do – this isn't over yet.

Today, with W/O Frewin and Haig, went to bomb petrol tanks at Rachid, the old Hinaidi. For the first time I put a stick bang on what I aim for, but 20lbers don't seem much good. Yesterday Dan and his boys put eighteen holes through the factory at Musaib (the one I missed). One Brushwood, here, who was attached to the

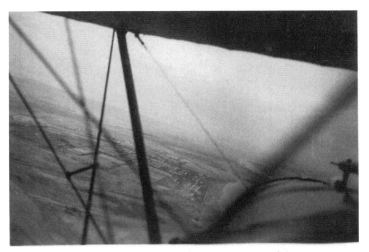

'Returning from a sortie'.
Habbaniya is below as Colin approaches to land.

Iraqi Air Force in some engineering capacity, knows exactly what is where in the target line. Much cooler today.

May 15th 1941

HABBANIYA

A RECCO PLANE VANISHES with Blackall and Ritz, pupils, on board. A Blenheim is attacked four times by an ME 110 at Mosul and six 109s are seen nearby in Northern Iraq. Five go off to drop leaflets on Falluja, which requires no small skill, and the prisoners' mail, addressed to the postmaster there. Yesterday I lead a formation to Rachid – Slack and Brown – but Slack cannot keep up and we go on alone. I miss my hangar but put four bombs through a house nearby, then overshoot with the next stick. Then last night I go up solo, from 2.15 to 4.30 am, half asleep all the time, and having nothing to do but think of MEs landing by moonlight and the first light of dawn.

A Bombay *(Bristol Bombay aircraft)* arrives from Egypt with a load of Marmite. We want guns here, not butter!

Today I do two half-hour patrols and shoot up some derelict cars on the desert road out of Ramadi. I spot seventeen lorries on the left bank of the Euphrates, opposite the ferry pier at Ramadi, and the boys go out to bomb them. Then I see a car on Falluja Plain. It sees me too, stops, and out get the passengers, being in too much of a hurry to shut the doors. I front gun the car, and notice the passengers are Arabs with rifles. I give one long burst, and I see one man lying in the sand and his body vanishes under the dust spurts, but he gets up afterward and runs off. I go down on another, but the Vickers jams, and whilst clearing it, I think this game is hardly cricket, so push off home and leave them.

May 16th 1941

HABBANIYA

I HAVE JUST TAKEN OFF ON A RECCO with Tiny and look back to see smoke over the camp, and three Heinkels high in the air. One is lagging behind, with a Gladiator on its tail. The Gladiator is then shot down, and we see the pilot bail out. The parachute fails to open properly and we go low over his body and the plane, which had exploded in mid-air. We return and report it and see one Heinkel with smoke coming out of one engine. It isn't seen anymore. Most of the bombs fall on the supply depot. Then off I go on recco and see some dust on the desert track north of Ramadi.

It's three lorries full of sacks which I machine gun and Tiny rear guns. I try some bombing and only get within fifteen yards – what the RAF call "in the target area", and blow up one of the drivers who is lying nearby. I return and report and Gordon Arthur goes and bombs them and sets them on fire, going so low that bits of 20lber hit his plane. He is the man who blew an Iraqi troop's topee off with his slipstream in the Battle of the Plateau. Then six

'A gladiator burning after a raid'. Habbaniya polo ground.

MEs get Reggie Wall, but the story is a bit confused and he is in hospital, not dead thank God. I didn't shoot at those drivers, Iraqi troops in uniform, but Tiny did. I don't like ring and head, would much rather an Aldis sight.

I am drinking too much - lime juice and water etc - and have had no exercise, bar two half-hour walks, since this little war began.

May 17th 1941

HABBANIYA

SAW REGGIE WALL, who has a lot of superficial holes in him. He was testing a plane and doing a wide circuit when six ME110s caught him over Dhibban. He did a crash landing somewhere, got out and ran for shelter and they dropped a bomb near him. The ambulance, which had been collecting the body of young Hertage in that Gladiator, saw it and stopped for him, and was machine-gunned by the Hun.

Reggie had sent off a letter to Group Captain Bussell, telling him of our plight, as far as training was concerned, and that I had been saying that I ought to go back to the Frontier and the Army. Some lads, including Broadhurst, have now produced stories about the "Army officers having had it" and having applied to go back to the Army. Some people are damn swine.

Tiny and I had a drink with young Stoney this morning. Three Hurricanes arrived yesterday, to everyone's delight. Today two Gladiators shoot down two ME110s as they are taking off from Rachid aerodrome.

May 19th 1941

HABBANIYA

ANOTHER ME110 DAMAGED AT RACHID. A new AOC arrives, Air Vice Marshal D'Albiac, who evacuated from Greece and so knows his stuff. Old Smart had a slight car crash and packed it in with shock.[1]

Yesterday a proper operation order came out, for the investment of Falluja by Levies and the King's Own on the Plain (going there at dawn in Valencias). The RAF are then to bomb the hell out of it, the bombing being interspersed with pamphlets, until the troops there surrender. I have two salvoes, miss the cemetery and brick kiln, and nearly get taken off the show, as they all land in the desert. Then I put four through the bazaar roof, and four bounce off its walls, so I get a bullseye. Dropping from 4000 feet to 2000' and then releasing at 1000 feet seemed to do the trick. But the town hasn't surrendered, and no one thought of what to do if they didn't, at least the army didn't, so the AOC has now ordered them to capture Falluja.

The "Phantom Column" has arrived, and is dispersed about the Rest House with its M.T.[2]

May 20th 1941

HABBANIYA

RACHID IS BLASTED AT DAWN THIS MORNING. Cremin arrives late and we take off in the dark and get lost. I never find the squadron, so go straight there myself, reckoning on being safe, as there are Gladiators about. Bombing not much good. A Heinkel, or Savoia, does a photography run this morning, and on the way back drops a bomb or two. I go for a walk this afternoon and three more come over and blast the hangers. These are followed shortly by four ME110s who come down front gunning. They had a crack at the Harts on the race course this morning, so they must hang about here all day.

One general, twenty officers and five hundred men are captured in Falluja yesterday. Iraqi air force strength on 2nd May:- 24 "Peggy" Audaxes, 15 Northrops, 7 Gladiators, 4 Bredas, 4 Vincents, 3 Savoias, 5 odds and sods. Total 62. Frewin went out yesterday with some civilian to find a convoy at H1-3, and saw some MEs ground strafing, so came right home.

May 22nd 1941

HABBANIYA

NO FLYING YESTERDAY. Two ME110s come over and shoot up a Douglas on the ground belonging to Dudley Withers and Dickie Bird, who are here. I take them to the Club last night, and I find Dudley is engaged. This morning woken up at 5 am, as Falluja

205

is being attacked, and Haig, Figgis and self go off. I put a stick amongst some lorries and miss two cars going flat out, with two bombs apiece. Front gun jams so I have to come home, quarter of an hour after the other two, to find the camp being bombed, and 110s just finished and they all think I have "gone for a Burton", as the expression is here.

Off we go again and we spot the Iraqi troops attacking Falluja. I find a lot in holes and a road cutting, with two lorries under desert-coloured hoods. I miss them with both sticks, but reckon I got some troops. I nearly fail to pull out of the second dive. Then down with the Vickers and two long, long bursts at the troops, who sit up and fire their rifles at me. Then number three stoppage[1] so off home. The first sortie I got a number one every time after about fifteen seconds. A pity, as I had a runabout at my mercy, filled with troops with white hat bands crouching on the floor and hanging on the footboards. I always cut my knuckles on these damn bomb levers, and a bad one today.

[1] *The Lewis gun was notoriously prone to jamming, with three types of stoppages.*

May 23rd 1941
Habbaniya

I DO TWO MORE TRIPS OVER FALLUJA. One to bomb lorries at Khan Nukta police post, where I put a stick bang on the road, and the other to attack 100-200 troops who had come up to Falluja by the canal road south of the town. They had left their lorries and were sitting out in the open, so I spread out the bombs and cause a minor retreat of a few hundred yards. I believe they were all lying down on their faces with their rifles pointing in the air. Then the Sergeant Major would watch us come over and order "fire", and every man would pull his trigger with his thumb and a fusillade of shots would come into the air.

A aerial recce photo of Al Rashid air base, dated April 1941, used for raids in May.

At about 4.00 pm two bombs land in the Mess. One behind the C.O.'s quarters, some hundred feet from me, and the other one on the Mess lawn, five yards from our newest slit trench, which was full up at the time, though no one was injured. Also one through the roof of the depot NAAFI.

Reggie Wall is better, and now remembers doing a tight loop and a few aileron turns and getting one of the MEs in his sights. The King's Own have had three officer casualties yesterday, and the Iraqis had them forced back onto the bridge at one time. The local inhabitants also sniped them. Complaints that the Indian-made bayonets snapped off in the 8th body!

Germans dropped leaflets yesterday too, but from 11,000 feet or so. Two 110s over today, twice, but didn't fire, and reputed to have dropped a message on Air HQ.

May 25th 1941

HABBANIYA

TWO DOSES OF ME110S YESTERDAY, and the first finds us all in the tent and we all get hurt jumping into the same trench. Today a lackadaisical blitz on Ramadi, but I don't go up and haven't done so for two days now. Then some bombing by a lone Heinkel, and three 110s sweep by over the polo pitch and away. Cowley and I get the smoke candle and arrow working, but I doubt whether it will be of any use.[1]

Am fed up with this war. I get enough sleep, enough food and something cold to drink, but life is getting pretty monotonous and a lot of new chaps in the Mess whom I don't particularly want to talk with. But what to do.

[1] *A smoke candle was lit if the wind direction necessitated a runway change, to warn pilots coming in to land.*

May 27th 1941

HABBANIYA

I GO AND BOMB EMPTY PALM GROVES at Ramadi on the evening of the 25th, and then go off for a second trip. But the plane splutters during take off, so I throttle back, and long flames shoot out of the exhaust. I had opened the mixture control by mistake, according to Flt/Sgt Rhodes. Then up again to bomb the military school at Mushaid point, but bloody awful. Saw two flashes and two white puffs of smoke on the ground, so presume it was A/A fire, which Figgis (in the back) said he felt.

Heinkels at 0650 yesterday, but today's dose not yet delivered. Blenheims continually firing up Mosul. *(where the Luftwaffe contingent of ME110s and Heinkels were based.)* Met Masters[1] of 2/4 GR in the Club last night, shooting a line about battles round Basra. Went over with Dickie Cleaver and Allan after dinner, or "rations", to the cricket pitch to see Hugh Thomas and the boys and his Levy company there. Had a few whiskies, and we discuss hearsay tales of this war, and decide how it should be won. I must write to Ma again, but am too idle. A lot of funny fellows arrive in Blenheims here and recount their experiences in Greece innumerable times.

[1] *John Masters, who had served in Waziristan, and who later became a well-known novelist.*

May 29th 1941

HABBANIYA

YESTERDAY "KINGCOL" ADVANCED ON BAGHDAD. A canal had been dug across the road at Khan Nuqta, and the road flooded further down beyond that. We stand by all day to support them, but only one flight required, to attack some 1500-3000 tribesmen massing south of Falluja Plain. These turned out to be sheep.

Today Arthur, White and self go off to attack enemy "targets" in front of our advance guard, some 10-12 miles down the road from Khan Nuqta. We have as escort, one Gladiator flown by W/C Wrightman, and before we arrive he is attacked by three CR42s. We break formation and go down on the deck and see him shoot one down, the pilot sort of stepping out in his parachute, like going down in a lift. We fly low over him and his burnt-out plane and he looks a bit dago-ish in long trousers and a shirt, holding up his hands in surrender. We had previously seen what we thought were

Audaxes ground strafing, but which were really CR42s pulling out after diving on Wrightman.

I attack some lorries and miss each time, and White puts them on fire. I machine gun one, and then see our troops creeping forward and mortar smoke and explosions on the edge of a wood, so go down to look for a target in it. Am below 1000 feet when a burst comes up by my left elbow. It is deflected by a Lewis gun drum, but wounds my gunner, Williams, in the back. Only a deep graze I think, but I push off home, to find the whole squadron waiting anxiously on the polo ground as we are a long time away, and CR42s had been reported there during our absence. My bombing is getting bad again.

May 31st 1941

HABBANIYA

THE PILOT WAS CAPTURED, an Italian who had flown from Rhodes only the day before. He said the Wops had relieved the Germans in this country, so that's why no Messersmiths (sic) had been about lately. Yesterday went and bombed Washash Camp, across the Iron Bridge and near the King's Palace at Baghdad. I put a stick between the ends of two long barracks, hitting both, then four 20lb bombs through the roof of another one. One Sanderson in a Gladiator force landed some days ago on Falluja Plain and walked in by night through Iraqi patrols. The Levies refused to admit him by the wire, so he had to spend the night in the graveyard, with all the new Iraqi unburied dead.

Rachid Ali departed for Persia, and the new Government gave back the Ambassador his wireless to send a message asking for peace terms. Letter from Bill. C.O. said we would go to an Operational Training Unit in Egypt, and the other boys to do their Intermediate training in Rhodesia!

June 2nd 1941

BAGHDAD TAKEN AND ARMISTICE GRANTED. Germans supposed to have arrived with fifty and to have left with twenty-two planes. An ME110 found on the ground today, and one Blenheim vanished on recco two days ago. Dan announced today the dissolution of the squadron and final dissolution of 4 FTS. The Audaxes are to be flown to Egypt, and instructors probably to form a fighter and bomber squadron here.

Nigen Gribbons turns up last night, his regiment being Brigade reserve out near the hotel by the lakeside. Bob May and I drive him back, slightly intoxicated, then stop for supper there, just like old Frontier days – eaten in a bare tent under a new moon. Stonhill back from captivity, having been taken up to Kirkuk and seen some Germans there. Thirty-seven prisoners returned, including John Addy.

June 6th 1941

HABBANIYA

31 SQUADRON ARRIVED HERE. Dougie Homes, Bird and O'Neil staying here, the rest in the AHQ Mess. They bring the 'onlooker' with them. Met one Walters, RIASC, at the swimming pool who left 56th in 1937. He said Willie Armstrong has a staff job in the Shatt-el-Arab hotel in Basrah. Nine Harts and nine Oxfords have gone to Egypt, but Allan (Haig) and I are still here. Germans, in French-type machines, raid Amman yesterday, so it won't be long before they are here.

Looked over an ME110 in a hanger today, built in 1940. Flew a Hart from the racecourse, to the main 'drome, and also gave it an air test. Nothing registered on the ASI (airspeed indicator) and it was a more frightening trip than any I did in this war. Landed with some engine and a good drop! – but she stayed down.

June 13th, 1941

YESTERDAY I GO UP IN A BLENHEIM with Stonhill down to Basrah. A drink at the airport, and then off to see Willie Armstrong at Force HQ, whilst Stony goes to the RAF station. Willie very busy, and only able to have a few words with him, but he says 56th still in Wana, Maitland France is with the 59th in Palestine, and Abbot's on a parachutist course at home. Then on to Shaibah, very hot and reminiscent of Manzai.

Lunch with Kenneth Smith in the Mess, and they have a skull on the mantelpiece with a plate on it "The winner of the high diving competition 19 – "

Return after lunch and I drive for a bit, but bloody awful and I can't keep on a straight course. Today they decide to send us to Egypt, and eventually Rhodesia for an ATS course, so Allan and I fix ourselves up with a Hart each. If we get there I expect I shall be discovered, *(that he had cheated on his eyesight test to join the RAF)*, but shall have seen a bit of the world beforehand. One can't take much in the back of a Hart, and I shall most likely be landed with a passenger at the last moment. More kit to lose!

Glossary

The diaries are full of acronyms, abbreviations, military names and words in Urdu and Pashto. Below is a list of the most common:

2/13 G.R. – 2nd battalion, 13th Gurkha Rifles etc.
Bearer - an officer's personal servant, paid for by the officer.
B.O. – British Officer.
B.O.R. - British other ranks.
Babu – Indian orderly.
Badmash – bad man.
Bde – Brigade – typically 2-5 Battalions, up to 5000 soldiers.
Bn – Battalion, 800-1200 soldiers.
C.O. – Commanding officer.
Chapao - night raid.
Chaplies – leg protectors at ankle height.
Charpoy – boy servant.
Chota peg - a measure of spirits, usually whisky.
Column – an Battalion size expedition, large sortie.
Coy – Company – a unit of 100-200 soldiers.
CR42 - Italian Air Force Fiat Falcon, single seater fighter. •
Dogras – Indian troops from the Jammu region, serving in the British Indian Army.
Dushman – a local tribesman.
Fils - lowest denomination of Iraqi money.
Gasht - trek, expedition on foot.
I.O. – Indian officer.
I.O.R. – Indian other ranks.
Jhil - a small lake.
Khasadar – locally raised militia.
Khel - Wazir village or clan.
Khud - a ravine.
Lashkar – rebel, insurgent or group of them.
Levies - Assyrian militia serving as RAF guards in Iraq.

ME109 - Luftwaffe Messerschmitt Bf 109 fighter.
ME110 - Luftwaffe Messerschmitt Bf 110 fighter-bomber.
M.G. – machine gun.
M.T. - motor transport.
Munshi - a secretary, or language teacher.
NCO - non-commissioned officer.
Nullah – stream, dry river bed, gully.
P.A. – Political administrator or agent (like local governor).
Pani - water.
Picquet – forward observation post, sometimes spelled picquet.
R.A. – Royal Artillery.
R.P. – Reconnaissance Patrol.
R.T.R. – Ready to Return, less often Royal Tank Regiment. •
R.U.R. – Royal Ulster Rifles.
Rajputs – 7th Rajput Regiment.
Razcol – Waziristan campaign army, named after Razmak. •
RIASC – Royal Indian Army Service Corps.
RMC - Royal Military College, Sandhurst.
Rs - rupees.
RSM – Regimental Sergeant Major.
Sangar – defensive position, normally sandbagged.
Scouts – locally raised militia.
Shikara - guide, hunter.
Shikhari - lake boat.
U/S - unserviceable.
ULIA – Unattached list, Indian Army
V.B. – Vickers-Berthier light machine gun.
Wimpey - Wellington bomber.

Further reading

The Big Little War

For wider context on The Battle of Habbaniya - see May 1941 entries in these diaries - read James's history 'The Big Little War.' This is the incredible true story of how a handful of RAF trainee pilots (including Colin) and their instructors, in antiquated biplanes, defeated the Iraqi army and the Luftwaffe, to save Britain's Middle East empire. Based in part on this volume of the diaries.

The War Diaries of Colin Dunford Wood, Vol 2, 1942-44

Volume two of the war diaries covers operations in the air in Burma, flying Lysanders, Hurricanes and Spitfires. Heart-stopping moments include flying the last Hurricane out of Burma in advance of the advancing Japanese, and being shot down into a crocodile swamp by friendly fire.

The War Diaries of Colin Dunford Wood, Vol 3, 1944-46

Volume three of the war diaries covers training back in the UK, flying Spitfires in support of the Rhine Crossing in 1944, postwar life in Holland in 1945, and numerous romantic adventures - before finally getting his girl...

About the Editor

James Dunford Wood has worked in films and e-commerce, and as a publisher, travel writer and author. www.jdwoodbooks.com

Last, if you have enjoyed these diaries, please leave a review on Amazon!